INVESTIGATIVE REPORT WRITING MANUAL

FOR

LAW ENFORCEMENT

AND SECURITY

PERSONNEL

Police and Fire Publishing

1800 N Bristol St, Ste C408

Santa Ana, Ca. 92707

e-mail: steve@policeandfirepublishing.com

www.policeandfirepublishing.com

ISBN: 978-0-9821157 0-1

ABOUT THE AUTHORS

Sandra Machuga, the original author of this book, is a veteran of 19+ years in law enforcement. She retired from the Cypress Police Department in 1994 as a Sergeant. During her law enforcement career she served in patrol, investigations, crime prevention and community relations, and as a school resource officer, and was the recipient of numerous commendations and awards, among them Officer of the Year. She received a Bachelor's Degree in Criminal Justice Administration from California State University, Fullerton, a Master's Degree in Public Administration from the University of Southern California, and a Community College Lifetime Teaching Credential from the State of California.

Her experience includes: teaching for over 20 years at basic police academies, advanced officer training programs, and community colleges in Southern California, including Rio Hondo, Whittier, Golden West, Huntington Beach, Orange County Sheriff's Department, Fullerton, and Cerritos. She is presently on staff at Fullerton Police Academy/Administration of Justice Program, Fullerton Community College, in Fullerton, California where she teaches Investigative Report Writing and Investigation of Homicidal Behavior.

Pete Bollinger is a sergeant with the Santa Ana Police Department with 20 years of law enforcement experience. He has worked in the Personnel Section and most recently in the Prosecution Unit filing cases that ranged from low-level infractions to murder. His interaction with the district attorney's office was invaluable in gaining a perspective of the pertinent information necessary to file a case.

Steve Winston is a background investigator with the Santa Ana Police Department. He has conducted thousands of background investigations and completed the associated administrative reports.

You will be the beneficiary of a collaboration of these individuals in creating a new and improved Investigative Report Writing Manual. Study and practice the exercises dedicating yourself to the lifelong goal of 'being better tomorrow than you were today'.

INVESTIGATIVE REPORT WRITING MANUAL

FOR

LAW ENFORCEMENT & SECURITY PERSONNEL

TABLE OF CONTENTS

AUTHOR'S NOTE

Basic investigative report writing concepts, whether for private security or for law enforcement, rarely change, but formats often do. Therefore, it makes sense to teach formats that are widely accepted. Most of the concepts discussed in this manual are consistent with reports from other professions. The Commission on Peace Officer Standards and Training (P.O.S.T.) has established guidelines for investigative report writing, and this manual emphasizes those concepts and standards.

In this manual we have attempted to address the most frequently recurring problems officers seem to have with their report writing. Contents of this manual are a result of many years of report writing instruction to law enforcement and private security personnel. A good report is the direct result of the officer's investigation. Report writing and investigative techniques go hand-in-hand. You can't have one without the other, so we made it a point in this manual to address the investigative steps necessary for a superior police report.

Officers should ALWAYS consult with their own organization and/or local prosecutor for clarification of any local laws and/or policies. This is especially critical when establishing the elements of the crime, and following the procedures for handling a particular investigation.

The goal of report writing is to tell the reader specifically what happened. If you understand that every complete sentence should have a noun and a verb, you're halfway to that goal. If you understand the concept of chronological order and its importance in painting an accurate picture of what occurred, you're three quarters of the way there. And if anyone with a basic high school education can read and understand your report, you're almost home. Writing simple, descriptive sentences and paragraphs completes the picture. Practicing the techniques outlined in this manual will result in a superior performance.

We will do our best to make you a better report writer. We have developed a variety of exercises that are intended to increase your level of competency. The exercises range from basic grammar and report writing to investigation and interviewing techniques. They are designed to both keep you interested and to encourage the acquisition of basic knowledge and the fundamentals of report writing. You will not be hired in law enforcement unless you write well because your reports are a reflection on you and the department.

INVESTIGATIVE REPORT WRITING MANUAL

FOR

LAW ENFORCEMENT AND

SECURITY PERSONNEL

CHAPTER 1

HOW REPORTS ARE USED

In this chapter, you will learn what makes an excellent report and how reports are used:

- *as a basis for criminal cases; as a basis for civil cases, including insurance, health department, risk management, or environmental (AQMD)*
- *as a source of statistical information*
- *to supply information to newspapers and the media*
- *to evaluate the officer*
- *by various reviewing audiences*
- *to document different types of incidents*

WHAT MAKES AN EXCELLENT REPORT

An excellent report is one that is well-written, and is identified by six basic, necessary qualities. A well-written report is:

1) Factual

2) Accurate

3) Clear

4) Concise

5) Complete

6) Timely

Deficiency in any of these areas cast doubts upon the capabilities of the officer who wrote the report.

"Report writing ability" refers not just to writing skills, but to the totality of skills—perceptual, analytical, information processing and language—that work together to produce a written document.

Factual: The report contains only facts. A fact is a thing that has actually happened or that is really true.

Accurate: The report is free from mistakes or errors. It is precise. It is exact.

Clear: The report is free from confusion and ambiguity and is easily understood.

Concise: The report states much in (relatively) few words by removing all expanded or superfluous details.

Complete: The report includes all necessary information: such as who, what, when, where, why and how. All of the elements of the crime are also included in the report.

Timely: The report should be completed as soon as possible.

Additional characteristics of a well-written report:

Grammatically Correct: The report has been written using the proper form and arrangement of words and sentence structure.

Legible: The report has been put down on paper in handwriting or printing that is readable, that can be read or deciphered easily. Legibility means writing or printing that is not "chicken scratch" or indecipherable "scribbling." Can the reader easily tell what the words are?

Objective: The writer has not injected his or her own bias or prejudice into the report.

MOST COMMON UTILIZATION OF REPORTS

Criminal and Civil Cases

Reports are written to document events. For law enforcement agencies, such documentation is important for future criminal prosecution as well as for liability in future civil litigation. In their original form, the reports are reviewed by detectives and supervisors, then read by the prosecuting and defense attorneys. Typically, the district attorneys base their decisions to file criminal charges on the contents of the original reports. These reports are also used to coordinate additional criminal investigations.

Reports can assist detectives in identifying methods of operations (M.O.), certain crime trends, and can link similar or related crimes and criminal activity together in an attempt to identify the perpetrator.

Reports are frequently used to assist officers and other participants to refresh their memories for testifying in court.

For private security companies, reports most often tend to be used to document events by which the client could or would be affected. Incidents such as slip-and-fall accidents, crimes, internal losses, etc., are issues that cost the client money, and therefore, are directly affected by the effectiveness of the security company and its personnel. Adequate documentation in such cases can save both the client and the security company time and money.

Of course, similar investigation and documentation are requirements in other professions, too. Professionals such as insurance investigators, private investigators, risk management investigators, human resources personnel, health department inspectors, code enforcement officers, etc., all deal with volatile incidents that could potentially expose an organization or individual to financial liability as well as harm the reputation of that organization or individual.

Statistical Information

Statistics compiled weekly, monthly, and yearly help local law enforcement agencies determine how to better allocate resources and to justify their activities. States collect their own crime statistics, which are then published yearly. Nationally, law enforcement agencies report certain criminal incidents to the Federal Bureau of Investigation, which then publishes a yearly report on all criminal activity within the country. This statistical information, along with the actual reports, provides evidence that the agency is meeting the needs of the community.

Newspapers and Other Media

In most instances, crime reports are available to radio, television and newspaper representatives. Much of what these organizations report is based upon the information contained in the report.

Officer Evaluation

Supervisors commonly use an officer's reports to judge how well the officer does his or her job. The report provides information about the officer's abilities, education, training, and deficiencies. An officer's reports reveal to a supervisor how an officer organizes his or her thoughts.

Reviewing Audience

In addition to being used within the agency, reports are commonly read by other parties such as:

- Regulatory and Law Enforcement Agencies (code enforcement, Department of Justice, and Department of Motor Vehicles.)

- Court Staff (prosecution and defense attorneys, judges, and clerical staff)

- Administrators (city, county, and state officials)

- Insurance Companies (attorneys, investigators, and clerical staff)

- Jurors (in both civil and criminal trials)

- Media (newspaper, television, and radio reporters)

TYPES OF REPORTS

A report is a written document characterized by a particular style and format, which describes an event or incident, thereby providing information. It can be said that the report is a formal statement or official account. Most organizations use specific printed forms on which to record information; these forms may sometimes be on computer disks or hard-drives as report templates.

Reports vary according to how they are used and why they are written. Here are some of the different types of reports:

Arrest Report: An arrest report is written whenever a person is arrested. This report must include the probable cause for the detention, arrest, and disposition of the suspect.

Clearance Report: A clearance report states the end result to a specific case. It might be the arrest of a suspect, the recovery of property, or the filing of a complaint. It brings the case to a conclusion.

Crime Report: A crime report is written after the investigating officer concludes that a crime has occurred. A crime report must include all the elements of the crime and should include all information regarding the crime at the time the report was taken, such as location, the time and place the crime occurred, loss or injuries, evidence collected, suspect description, etc. A crime report form tends to be a generic pre-printed form that can be used to document any criminal occurrence.

Event or Incident Report: An event or incident report is used to document events not considered criminal. Such events may be medical aid calls, civil disputes, citizen assists, and the like. Some agencies call these Service or Miscellaneous reports.

Evidence Collection Report: An evidence collection report establishes the chain of evidence, such as who discovered the evidence, when and where it was located, who collected it, and its disposition.

Memorandum: A memorandum is generally used to request information or to answer a request for information. It is less formal than the crime or incident report but can be just as important. Memorandums are commonly used to pass on information from shift to shift, to document minor disciplinary actions, vacation requests, training information, etc.

Narcotic, Drunk Driving, Intoxication Report: A narcotic, drunk driving, or intoxication report is used to describe the suspect's condition of being under the influence of a drug or alcohol. Most often, these are separate reports and written in conjunction with a crime report.

Officer's Activity Report or Daily Log: The activity report or daily log is commonly used to provide an agency with statistical information regarding the activity on an officer's shift. These reports include the calls the officer responded to, the disposition of the call, the amount of time spent on the call, and other activities within the shift such as car stops, number of citations written, etc. Some agencies obtain the same information via a computer terminal in the officer's vehicle.

Supplemental Report: A supplemental report is typically written by an officer other than the original reporting officer. For instance, an officer may assist a fellow officer in an investigation by interviewing people or by recovering property. The assisting officer would write a Supplemental Report to document his or her actions.

Traffic Collision Report: A traffic collision report provides information regarding traffic collisions. Such reports typically include statements of drivers and witnesses, diagrams, and photographs.

Traffic Citations: Given when a traffic or parking violation has occurred. They are pre-printed forms.

CHAPTER 2

INTERVIEWING AND NOTE TAKING

In this chapter you will learn about:

- *Interviewing and note taking*
- *Conducting the interview*
- *Audio and video tape recordings*
- *Crimes in progress*
- *Obstacles to overcome in interviews*
- *General guidelines for victim interviews*
- *Evaluating the suspect's demeanor and mental capacity*

BASIC INTERVIEWING AND HOW TO TAKE INTERVIEW NOTES

One of the most common mistakes officers make while interviewing victims, witnesses, and suspects is that the officers try to write down every word the person says. In many instances, this is unnecessary and extremely time-consuming. For most officers, it becomes very frustrating because they miss bits and pieces of information, which requires that the person being interviewed repeat statements again and again. This becomes frustrating for the person being interviewed, too.

There is a difference between an *interview* and an *interrogation*. We typically *interview* victims and witnesses to gather information. We *interrogate* suspects in an attempt to obtain incriminating statements such as *admissions* and *confessions*.

The word **note** is defined as a brief statement of factual experience, written down for review, as an aid to memory. Keeping that in mind, most people simply can't write quickly enough to note every word a person says. Therefore, a good note taker must be a good listener, too, which enables the listener to pick out descriptive words within speech. The descriptive words are written down in notes.

In an ideal world of police report writing victims, witnesses, and suspects would say only what the police officer wants and needs to hear to complete the narrative portion of the report. In that ideal world the victims, witnesses, and suspects would supply all the necessary information regarding items, places, descriptions, costs, and exact details of crimes. They would not ramble and discuss ideas that are not related to the crime being reported. In reality, the statements that the victims or witnesses volunteer often contain information that the officer cannot and should not use in the report narrative. This may include what somebody read in the newspaper yesterday about a similar crime or the victim's opinion about the crime.

The job of the reporting officer is to learn to separate relevant information from irrelevant information during the process of gathering the statements. Since the reporting officer often functions in an environment that may be tense and confused—victims and witnesses are typically upset as they make their

Statements—this is often an extremely difficult task. In addition, victims often do not understand exactly what the reporting officer needs in order to complete the narrative.

> ***ALWAYS REMEMBER:*** IF YOU DON'T ASK SPECIFIC QUESTIONS, YOU PROBABLY WON'T GET SPECIFIC ANSWERS!

Early in your career, you should acquire an understanding of how to take notes and how to interview. That understanding will make conducting interviews easier and more productive.

General rules concerning interviews are:

- Separate parties immediately.
- Do not allow parties to talk to one another.
- Do not allow parties to hear what is said during your interview (of any other party).

Note taking tips:

- Use abbreviations. Review the list of abbreviations in Chapter 6 to help shorten your notes.
- Don't try to write down every word that is said. Try to be selective; focus on what information you'll need to write an accurate report.
- Use a small, pocket-sized notebook to take notes, which will encourage you to be brief. —Remember, you can polish your language later.
- Restrict your notes to important facts. Headings can be used to highlight important sets of facts. —Details and less important facts can be added later, but while your memory is still fresh.
- Effective note taking requires the officer to alternate between listening and writing.
- Use last names when referring to victims, witnesses, and suspects, except in certain circumstances — (e.g., domestic violence case) where the suspect and victim may have the same last name. In those cases, use first name and last name.

Focus on descriptive words such as nouns and verbs. **WHO DID WHAT TO WHOM**? For example, if the victim says "My husband hit me with his fist" you should focus on **WHO**? (my husband) **DID WHAT**? (hit) **TO WHOM**? (me / with fist).

As you take notes, be more concerned with the accuracy of the information than with grammatical correctness. You will have time later, when you write the report, to edit for correctness. Your report must reflect what is in your notes. There should never be a conflict between the two. Use words, phrases, and sentence fragments that you know you can turn into complete sentences later.

Accurate notes will eliminate the need to re-contact involved parties to obtain information that was forgotten because the officer relied solely on memory. Accurate notes will provide a greater degree of accuracy regarding times, statements, and events and will assist the officer in refreshing his or her memory before testifying.

Keep in mind that the notebook is subject to the scrutiny of the court. The court can develop impeachable inconsistencies between reports and notes; therefore, non-police information should not be written in the notebook.

SAMPLE PAGE OF NOTES:

In your notes (and only in your notes), you can use your own abbreviations as long as you can always decipher them. Here is an example. On the left is a sample of what your notes might look like. On the right is what the notes actually say.

12/16/04	Date of Report: 12/16/04
V/DANIEL GEORGE WATSON	Victim's Name Victim's
10/11/65	Date of Birth Victim's
1200 MCFAY ST., ANA, 92805	Address Victim's Phone
714-688-0989	Number

LOCK/LEFT RES 8AM TODAY RET 3PM

FRT DOOR KICKED IN (FOOTPRINT)

LIVING RM TV $500

REAR MSTR BDRM RNSKD-0

LIVES ALONE

DRS/WIND STILL LOCKED

NO S/

The victim locked and left his residence at 8:00 a.m. this morning and returned at 3:00 p.m. this afternoon. When he got there he saw that the front door was open and that there was a shoeprint on the front door. He discovered that the TV in the living room was gone. The TV is valued at $500. The victim found that the rear master bedroom had been ransacked but that nothing had been taken. The victim lives alone.

I (investigating officer) found all the other doors and windows still locked. There is no known suspect.

CONDUCTING THE INTERVIEW

Early in your career it is best to establish some type of system or procedure when you interview victims, witnesses or suspects. You will hear many theories on the best way to gather information and we will provide one in this workbook. Optimally, you should interview the same way every time. There are exceptions to this rule, but generally: *Listen, Write, and Review!*

The reality is everyone in law enforcement has a slightly different opinion on the way to write a report. That in itself is not an issue; go to a bookstore and observe the thousands of books on the shelves and no two books will be alike. Your training officer/supervisor/sergeant/lieutenant or any other authority will have his/her own theory and it is important to your future that you realize they are in charge. While you are under their tutelage, do what they tell you to do. After you have completed the training process take the best from each trainer and incorporate it into your style.

You are what you write! You will be judged by detectives and administrators on your investigation, interview, and how well you write. They will label you as an inept, competent, or superior report writer. If you become known as a superior report writer, your career will ascend up the ranks at a faster pace if you choose to take that route; detectives will appreciate the completeness and clarity of your reports and more cases will be filed by the prosecutor.

First step: Have the person tell you what happened, but don't take any notes. This is your opportunity to develop a rapport with the person. Let them tell the story in their own words. Control the interview. *Listen* to what the person says and while doing so, note in your mind the additional information you will need to clarify or information that requires further details.

Second step: Take your notebook out and have the person tell you the story again while you ask questions. This will give you time to *Write* important words and phrases down while keeping the person on track and not veering off on an unrelated topic. If you need to tell the person to slow down, do so.

Finally: *Review* with the person the information that you've written down. This will give both of you an opportunity to correct any information that was incorrectly noted.

Interview people this way each and every time and chances are you won't miss important information. Certainly, the primary goal of your report and investigation serves to promote justice: if a crime has been committed, the report needs to give the relevant information to lead to a possible investigation and ultimately, to a conviction. If no crime has been committed, the report needs to reflect that.

WHO, WHAT, WHEN, WHY, WHERE, AND HOW

Here are some questions that will help to ensure that all necessary information is obtained:

WHO

Who was the victim?

Who was the complainant?

Who discovered the crime?

Who saw or heard anything of importance?

Who had a motive for committing the crime?

Who committed the crime?

Who had the means to commit the crime?

Who had access to the crime scene?

Who searched for, identified, and gathered evidence?

The evidence was turned over to whom?

With whom did the victim associate?

With whom was the victim last seen?

With whom do the witnesses associate?

With whom did the suspect commit the crime?

Who helped the perpetrator?

WHAT

What crime was committed?

What are the elements of the crime?

What were the actions of the suspect before and after the crime?

What actually happened?

What do the witnesses know about it?

What evidence was obtained?

What was done with the evidence?

What weapons were used?

What action did the officers take?

What further action should be taken?

What knowledge, skill or strength was needed to commit the crime?

What other agencies were notified?

What other agencies need to be notified?

Which witnesses were not interviewed?

What time was the crime reported?

What time did the officers and the investigators arrive?

What time were the witnesses interviewed?

What type of transportation was used in committing the crime?

What was the motive for the crime?

What weapons were used?

What type of property was taken/damaged?

What other crime could be associated with this one?

WHEN

When was the crime committed?

When was it discovered?

When were the authorities notified?

When did officers arrive at the scene?

When was the victim last seen alive?

When was the arrest made?

When did witnesses hear anything unusual?

When did the suspect decide to commit the crime?

WHY

Why was the crime committed?

Why was the particular weapon/tool used?

Why was the crime reported?

Why was the crime reported late?

Why were witnesses reluctant to give information?

Why is the suspect lying?

Why did the suspect commit the crime when she/he did?

WHERE

Where was the crime committed?

Where was the crime discovered?

Where was the entry made?

Where was the exit?

Where was the weapon obtained that was used to commit the crime?

Where was the victim found?

Where was the suspect seen during the crime?

Where was the suspect last seen?

Where does/did the suspect live?

Where is the suspect now?

Where would the suspect likely go?

Where was the evidence found?

Where was the evidence stored?

HOW

How are the victim(s), witness(es) and suspect(s) related?

How do the victim(s), witness(es) and suspect(s) know each other?

How was the crime committed?

How did the suspect(s) leave the scene?

How did the suspect(s) obtain the information necessary to commit the crime?

 How was the crime discovered?

How was the weapon/tool from the crime obtained?

How was the weapon/tool used?

How was the crime reported?

How was the arrest made?

How much damage was done?

How much property or money was taken?

How much information is being withheld?

OBSTACLES TO OVERCOME IN INTERVIEWS

Difficult interviews

People react differently to being interviewed, depending upon the situation. Victims and witnesses who have witnessed a traumatic event, such as a shooting or robbery, may have difficulty relating information to you that you need for the report. It is your responsibility to take control of the interview and to assure the victim, in particular, that you are there to help her or him. By being responsive to the victim's physical and emotional needs during this time of crisis, the officer will obtain better information, increase the likelihood that the victim will cooperate with prosecution, improve community relations, and enhance victim recovery.

Witnessing a traumatic event places a person in a situation in which most people, including officers, are psychologically unprepared for. As a result, the senses perceive things differently than in a normal situation. It is very common for the efficiency of senses, such as sight and hearing, to be reduced by at least two-thirds, which means it takes longer for the brain to recognize what it is seeing or hearing. These changes cause a person to perceive sights and sounds differently than under normal circumstances. A gun being fired might sound muffled, time might be perceived as being much longer or shorter than what actually occurred, and colors might be seen as being extremely bright or dim. Traumatic events can alter the accuracy of information related in your report; you need to be prepared for this type of problem and should not necessarily interpret that the person being interviewed is deliberately giving you inaccurate information.

Many law enforcement situations are critical incidents that can result in crisis to the interviewed person. A critical incident is any situation which is a threat to the life or physical integrity of oneself, a loved one, or a person for whom you are responsible (e.g., employer/employee, parent/child, or officer/trainee) Examples of critical incidents are rape, death threat, severe auto accident, natural disaster, hate crime, domestic violence, child abuse, death notification, robbery, burglary, arson, theft, and missing person.

A crisis is an event or series of events that temporarily overwhelm a person's normal coping mechanism. Officers tend to be the first line of defense for a victim in crisis. Oftentimes, how the officer approaches the victim, and comforts and treats the victim, can alleviate much of the distress the victim will go through. Realizing the important role he or she plays, the officer should look for signs that the victim is in crisis. Feelings that a victim may reveal are helplessness, being out of control, powerlessness, anger, sadness, and fear. These feelings may manifest themselves in a variety of ways. The officer should look for the following physical responses commonly exhibited:

- Red flushed face
- Fixed stare
- Loud voice
- Hyperventilation; rapid breathing
- Rigid body
- Shaking; twitching hands; clenched fists
- Nausea
- Hesitation to move as directed
- Heart palpitation

Extreme responses are:

- Screaming; crying; hysterics
- Severe depression
- Rage
- Violence towards self, others or property
- Immobility (frozen)

A victim may say one thing and yet show the opposite response. For instance, they may be outwardly calm, but be trembling uncontrollably. They say they are not angry and yet clench their fists and lock their jaw.

GENERAL GUIDELINES FOR VICTIM INTERVIEWS

1. Introduce yourself by full name and title.

2. Explain your role and purpose.

3. Acknowledge the ordeal the victim has been through and reassure them they are safe; use a calm, reassuring, supportive tone of voice.

4. Determine whether the victim has any injuries and if needed, obtain necessary medical care.

5. Provide privacy for the victim during the interview.

6. Explain what you need to do and why before you do it—this includes describing procedures, explaining the reasons for questions that are asked, and informing the victim about how the information you are requesting will be used.

7. Allow the victim to relate what happened in his/her own words. Form an outline of the events as you listen. Follow the outline when you question the victim further to fill in the detail, e.g., to establish the elements of the crime and to obtain a description of the offender. Ask simple questions.

8. Validate the feelings and reactions the victim expresses as normal responses to victimization. Do not cut off the expression of these reactions.

9. Keep in mind that your goal is to obtain the cooperation of the victim. Give them choices and allow them to make decisions. They are not required to cooperate with your investigation.

10. Determine any special needs and immediate concerns of the victim and help with problem-solving. Be particularly alert to issues related to personal safety.

11. Prepare the victim for future reactions and feelings related to the victimization.

12. Mobilize support systems for the victim, such as friends, family, and crisis counseling.

13. Give the victim information about follow-up investigation procedures and resources available for additional help or information.

INTERVIEWING CHILDREN

One of the most difficult interviews an officer will ever be asked to do is an interview of a child who has been victimized. Children are also victims of abuse, sexual molestation, and domestic violence. As a result of these crimes, the child victim is traumatized and may have a difficult time telling an officer what exactly took place. Even though such interviews are difficult, they can be made easier if the officer is aware of a child's capabilities, and some DOs and DON'Ts when talking to them.

Language used with adults may not be interpreted the same way by a young child. Use language that a child understands and can relate to. Keep in mind that children react to tone of voice, body language, and facial expressions. They are easily influenced and easily swayed by leading questions. Because they seek approval and see you as an authority figure, if they see displeasure in your face or hear it in your voice, they may change their statements to please you. They can tell by the expression on your face that you don't believe them and may think that they've done something bad.

In most jurisdictions, allegations of child abuse, and child molestation will eventually be referred to your jurisdiction's social services agency. Where possible, get these organizations involved as quickly as possible in an attempt to limit the number of interviews the child must go through. In many jurisdictions it is commonplace for law enforcement, district attorney, and social services to have their representatives present at the interview so the child isn't put through repeated interviews unnecessarily.

Interviews should be conducted promptly. Children's recollection of events change as time goes by. Consider videotaping the interview.

Some guidelines when interviewing children are:

·   Arrange for a comfortable setting for the interview. If possible, interview them within their own homes so they feel more secure. Do not interview them in the same environment or setting where the abuse took place.

·   Get down to their level. Don't tower over them! Sit on the floor with them so you are eye-to-eye. Their hesitation in talking to you will probably be eased if you first take a few minutes to talk to them about school, their toys, playmates, etc., before asking questions relative to your investigation. By doing so, you not only put the child at ease but you can quickly assess their social, intellectual, and physical development.

·   In most instances, parents and guardians, should not be in attendance (especially when they could be the suspect(s)). They tend to inhibit the child from talking and oftentimes can't keep from interrupting and interfering in your interview. Try to have another officer present during the interview.

·   Explain who you are and tell the child why you are there: to protect and help. Assure them that they have done nothing wrong. Get on a first-name basis with the child as soon as possible and encourage the child to call you by your first name, not Officer so-and-so.

· Try to establish that the child understands the difference between a lie and the truth. Describe how you established that the child understands the difference.

· In cases of child molestation, use terminology that the child understands, such as "peepee," "boobies," etc. Have the child define for you exactly what they mean when they use such words. Have them point to objects so you understand. Do not assume that you know what the child is referring to. Dolls, even a stuffed toy, can aid you in having the child define various parts of the body. Drawings and pictures can also be of assistance.

· Determine from the child what type of language the suspect used.

· Avoid the use of "why" questions because most children will interpret such questions as being accusatory. In cases where the suspect is a relative, the child may feel he or she is going to get the suspect/relative in trouble and may hesitate.

· In the beginning of the interview, start with generic questions such as "How did you get the black and blue mark on your face?" rather than saying "Who hit you?" Ask "what happened next?" Although such questions may be somewhat open-ended and may add time to your interview, it allows the child to fill in the gaps with specifics.

· Keep in mind that children get bored easily. Take frequent breaks.

· Young children will have trouble with dates. They might be able to narrow down the time frame of incidents if they can use birthdays, holidays, etc. as a reference. Older children may even keep a diary. Have the child tell you about each individual incident. Each act committed is another count that can be filed against the defendant in court.

· If applicable to your investigation, ask the child if certain types of pictures, (sexually explicit), videos, etc., were shown to, or taken of the victim, or if books, magazines of that type were shown to him or her. Does the child know what happened to them or where they are kept?

EVALUATION OF DEMEANOR AND MENTAL CAPACITY

Occasionally, a question may arise regarding a suspect's mental capacity. It is unusual for district attorneys to question the ability of victims or witnesses to recollect events but most often this question arises with a defense attorney trying to establish a defense of diminished capacity. The question would focus on whether or not the suspect knew right from wrong at the time the offense was committed. Another question that can come into play is whether or not the suspect willingly waived her or his Miranda rights, which [waiver] subsequently led to incriminating statements.

An officer would be wise to consider the following questions and to make sure that these topics are mentioned in the report. In each case, be specific in noting behavior and statements.

- Does the suspect speak rationally or irrationally?

- Does she or he answer straightforwardly or evade questions?

- Is the response to questioning intelligent or does it seem confused?

- Does the suspect appear to have control over her or his actions?

- What is the suspect's emotional condition? (crying, depressed, happy, etc.)

- Does the suspect appear to be under the influence of alcohol or drugs? (type of alcohol, how much consumed in what span of time, type of drugs, prescription or not, etc.)

- Does the suspect give any reason for her or his actions?

- Note the suspect's appearance at the time of interview.

Officers can help to establish the suspect's demeanor at the time the offense was committed by asking the following questions of the victims and witnesses:

- What was the suspect's appearance at the time of the offense?

- How did the suspect act?

- Did the suspect scream or yell? What did the suspect say?

- How did the suspect commit the act?

- Was the suspect under the influence of drugs or alcohol?

- Did the suspect do or say anything during or after the crime?

Abused spouses

Domestic violence is one of the most common calls and reports you will handle. Emotions range from hysteria to learned helplessness and acceptance. The interview and how you approach it is crucial to establishing the elements of the crime. Immediately make the victim feel safe and that he/she can tell you the truth about what happened. If they are reluctant to divulge information, win their trust by offering programs and safe havens.

Get a statement from the suspect prior to arresting him/her. Officers will often spend an hour with the victim covering every detail of the incident, only to be told by the prosecutor the case will not be filed because it is his word against hers. A single sentence by the suspect will corroborate the victim's story and result in a conviction.

Rape

I have read and heard hundreds of times that rape victims should be interviewed by female officers; that may be true, but unfortunately, this is not possible as the percentage of females on patrol is usually less than 5% of the patrol division. Whether you are male or female remain professional and respectful. There will be awkward moments during the interview, but the questions you must ask are vital to the case.

Molestation

Interviewing a child is difficult, but similar to the mentally challenged individual, you are their voice; possibly the only advocate they have. First, you must come down to their level. Any adult is an imposing figure to a child. In fact, you should have all of the adults other than a social worker or medical professional step out of the room. Then sit on the floor or crouch down to the child's level. Begin the interview by introducing yourself by your first name. Ask them about school, friends, toys, etc…this will help you determine their maturity level and willingness to talk to you. Make all the adults go away and advise the child you are there to protect them and that is what you will do.

Establish that they know the difference between the truth and a lie. This can be done with a few simple questions and subsequent answers from the child.

Children will use their own words for body parts; a penis might be called a "wee wee" or breasts might be called "boobies." Do not assume you know what body part they are speaking about. Use a doll or have them draw pictures. It may be beneficial to videotape the interview as the child may suppress or simply forget what happened to him/her.

Language

Occasionally you will run across a person that speaks a foreign language unknown to you. Usually when there is one who speaks the undecipherable language there are others in the area who can help. However, you must be aware of false translation or misinterpretation by the translator. Use all other information to determine what actually occurred. Another option is to call a translator through the dispatch 911 system; they can connect you with scores of translators who speak exotic and distant languages.

Deaf

The Americans with Disabilities Act (ADA) requires that every city be equipped to provide emergency services to the disabled. These services may not be available to you in the field. Consider these options:

- Pencil and paper is the most often used method. Though slow, it is accurate and creates a memorialized dialogue to book into evidence.
- Texting has risen in popularity and most young people will be able to do this.
- Laptops are readily available and can be utilized to create a running dialogue.

Mentally challenged

These are difficult interviews. Be patient and try not to get frustrated. The interview may become lengthy. Mentally challenged individuals frequently have special needs. They are often taken advantage of and have no recourse. You are their only hope.

Details

An easy way to get in the good graces of detectives is to inquire about details and to lock the subject into a statement. We will be discussing this more in the suspect interview section, but it is also important to lock in a victim and witness into a statement. They may be lying or become increasingly frightened as the case proceeds through the justice system due to intimidation.

Automatic pilot

After a while all reports will seem the same; to guard against that, maintain your work ethic and professional integrity. I was writing three or four reports a day on possession of a needle/syringe in one of our local parks. I was accustomed to writing that the arrestee had track marks (scars from injecting narcotics) on their forearms. I was embarrassed when testifying in court and had to explain why I wrote an inaccurate statement as the female I arrested was a new user and had no scarring. I was on auto pilot and learned a very valuable lesson; each report is a separate and individual case and deserves specific attention and dedication.

Contact information

Victims and witnesses can be difficult to locate. Obtain as many phone numbers, cell, work, home, Mother's, friends', etc...document any place they stay other than their primary residence; work address, friends addresses, neighbors, etc...

Remember the information you gather will be jumbled and out of sequence. It is up to you to write a report and display its contents in a chronological, logical and understandable way. The goal of each and every report is to serve justice and memorialize an event as each individual remembers it.

Interview of suspect/arrestee

Most young officers make this part of the investigation much more difficult than it really is. Abiding by the Miranda Decision is very simple. Miranda requires that an officer advise the arrestee of their right to remain silent, obtain counsel, etc...after being taken into custody. The television and movies show the arrestee being read Miranda Rights immediately upon being taken into custody. This rarely happens and in fact many officers do not read Miranda Rights at all. These particular officers argue, "He is going to lie anyway and if he wants to tell his side of the story he can tell it to the jury." What they do not realize is, locking a suspect into a statement does just that, "locks him in." The statement forces the defendant to abandon specific types of defenses, or admit he lied during the interview.

When a subject is out of custody and being interviewed, Miranda is not necessary. When the subject is in custody and you are not conducting any type of interrogation, you also do not need to offer Miranda Rights. I have heard of officers in the field stopping a confession to advise the remorseful out-of-custody subject of Miranda. This is ignorant and unforgivable.

Filing a case

There will often be no rhyme or reason for the filing of a case. Here is how it works:

The report

Officer writes the report and either makes the arrest or the detective follows up on the information and makes the arrest.

Filing the report

The report is delivered to the District Attorney's Office; a prosecutor will review the case and determine if there is enough evidence to convince a jury of twelve the person is guilty. This is generally not a reflection of your capabilities as they are weighing factors beyond your control such as "jury appeal." Cases will be refused for a variety of reasons and are usually labeled, "IOJ" in the "Interest of Justice."

Arraignment

If the case is filed, the arrestee is entitled to an arraignment within 48 hours of his/her arrest and a preliminary hearing within 10 calendar days.

Preliminary hearing

The arresting officer and/or detective will usually testify at the preliminary hearing and also speak for the victim and witnesses. The judge at the preliminary hearing will determine whether there is more evidence than not that the defendant committed the crime. The case is either set for trial or the defendant is released due to a lack of evidence.

Pre-trial

There will be pre-trials in which the prosecutor and defense attorney try to forge a deal to close the case.

Motions

A common delay tactic by the defense is to file a Motion to Suppress Evidence Hearing PC1538.5 It is similar to a preliminary hearing in which the officer will testify with only a judge present. The judge will determine if the evidence can be used at trial.

Trial

If a deal cannot be made the case will proceed to a trial by a judge or jury. A jury is comprised of twelve people who must unanimously decide on a guilty or not guilty verdict; otherwise it is declared a hung jury and mistrial. If a mistrial occurs the prosecutor decides whether or not to retry the case.

Polling the jury

Polling the jury is a term for speaking with the jurors after the case. Much can be learned by speaking with them and if you have the opportunity you should take it. Do not be defensive or accusatory or even try to tell them the truth. They will not understand and you will only validate their decision by acting in any manner less than professional.

The above sequence was generated by the report that you wrote. You may have been in court all day and then worked all night; the shift was busy and you waited until after the shift to finish the paperwork. None of these people will consider those factors when reading your product. Your competency will be judged on your finished product; once again, "you are what you write!"

Audio and video tape recording

Recordings of both types can help to eliminate questions as to how an interview or interrogation was conducted. Using a recorder can be a problem in that officers tend to include too much unnecessary information. Don't forget that these instruments can malfunction. Don't ever allow a tape recording to take the place of good notes! Take notes, as well as utilizing the recording device.

There are Penal Code sections (e.g., CPC 632 and 633) that govern the use of recordings. Review the applicable codes and restrictions as well as your organizations restrictions.

*When you **do** use recording devices, make sure that you always **include on the tape**:*

1) Your name, rank, and identification number

2) Department name, interview/interrogation date and time

3) Case number and type of case

4) Suspect's name and date of birth

5) Advisement of rights

The tape should be treated as evidence and booked into evidence accordingly. The tape can be transcribed, or you can paraphrase what was said in the taping in your report and then refer the reader to the actual tape recording for more information. Make sure that any break in the tape is explained in detail, such as "Suspect Jones was given a bathroom and coffee break from 1605 hours until 1615 hours."

Tape recordings are a double edged sword; they have both saved officers from trouble and verified wrong-doing. When you are a police officer, the public does not have an expectation of privacy; therefore, you can record anytime, anywhere. This is not the case for the general public. For example:

• Motor officers frequently tape their contacts to protect themselves from the many lies and false complaints the public makes.

• Patrol officers place two suspects in the back of a police car and record them.

• Detectives record phone conversations with suspects and on occasion have the victim call the suspect and record the conversation often leading to a prosecution.

• Phone calls from jail and prison are recorded and monitored.

Issues with recordings

Broken or dead space in the tape needs to be explained. On occasion an incident that is audio or video taped by an officer is flipped around and used as evidence against an officer. One department actually videotaped their use of force on a violent individual and was shocked when the general public viewed the incident as excessive force. This type of incident is rare, however, and the overwhelming majority of cases exonerate the officer during false complaints.

Anticipating defenses

Understand that your report being attacked in court does not mean you have written a poor report or are an incompetent investigator. Do your best to close down defenses, such as, "He dropped a bundle of a white powdery substance on the ground and I retrieved it." You can shut down several defenses with a line or two such as, "There were no other small white objects in the area." Or, "I walked directly to the bundle and picked it up." This will prevent the defense attorney from insinuating a mistake or a time delay. Experience will help you with closing defenses, but simple logic can place you ahead of the experience curve. There will be cases that will invite hard questioning by a defense attorney through no fault of your own. It may even be caused by exculpatory evidence that you included in your report. You, of course, should have done everything in your power to refute anything exculpatory, but simply report the facts even if they hurt your case.

The evidence, testimony and circumstances may be fragmented and difficult to prosecute. The defense attorney is only doing his/her job. If you lose a case because of circumstances beyond your control, do not take it personally. It is what it is! Always, and I repeat, **always tell the truth** even if you can feel the case leaning toward an acquittal.

If an officer places him or herself in the shoes of the District Attorney prosecuting a case, he or she will have a clear understanding for the need to anticipate any defense strategies that may occur during a trial. Often, if the officer had reflected on the incident being investigated and anticipated the possible defenses that the accused party might have used, he or she might have seen the importance of something that originally escaped notice. In fact, one of the most common complaints made by District Attorneys about police reports is that information is frequently absent from reports that allows accused individuals to effectively refute the assertion of guilt.

While it is important to include in your report information that documents a suspect's possible guilt and which anticipates possible defenses, it is equally critical that information which tends to show the accused innocent, (exculpatory information) also be included in the report. Your job as an investigating and reporting officer is to include all relevant information no matter how that information may portray the suspect. Never exclude exculpatory information in an effort to make a stronger case. Such action is unethical and may lead to disciplinary action.

CHAPTER 3

DESCRIPTIONS OF SUSPECTS AND PROPERTY

In this chapter you will learn how to:

- *Properly identify the parties*
- *Properly document suspect description*
- *Properly document property description*
- *Properly document the collection of evidence*
- *Properly use/convert the 24-hour clock*

IDENTIFYING THE PARTIES

Victim (V) - A person who suffers some loss or injury. (A business or a company may also be a victim)

Suspect (S) - A person who is believed to have committed the crime.

Witness (W) - A person who saw or can give a firsthand account of something.

Reporting Party (R/P) - A person who gives information.

Informant (I) - A person who gives information or serves as a source of information to law

enforcement, usually for something in return (e.g., money, leniency, etc.).

SUSPECTS

Suspect Description Checklist

When interviewing a victim, have them start at the suspect's head and work down to his/her feet. If a victim or witness has difficulty recalling information, tell them to close their eyes and to envision the suspect in their mind and then provide you with the information as noted below.

Refer to Appendix S, Sample Reports, which will provide additional samples of each heading.

Obtain:

Gender: Male or female.

Race: Descent is an identifier: white, black, Native American (Indian), Hispanic/ Latino, Asian.

Age: Give exact age, if known; if not known, use an approximation, such as 18-23 years.

Height: Use your own size as a measurement. Ask the witness to use your height as a comparison. Use approximation, with a range of 3- 4", such as 5"8" to 6"0".

Weight: Use your own size as a gauge. Ask the witness to compare the suspect's weight to your weight. Use approximation, with a range of 20-25 lb. such as 140-160 lb.

Build: Thin, stocky, muscular, athletic, heavy, overweight.

Scars: Location, design, and size.

Tattoos: Location, design, and size.

Peculiarities: Teeth: Missing, gold/silver, false, discolored, braces.

            Speech: Slurred, regional accent, foreign accent, stutter, lisp

            Limp: Cane / Crutches

            Amputations

            Body or facial disfigurement

Clothing: Styles: Western, formal, costume, specialty, military

Hair: Blonde, light brown, brown, black, red, gray, bald, bleached, salt and pepper, streaked (with what colors?).

Hair Style: Short, long, "permed," "corn rows," right/left part, pony tail, over ears, receding, balding, braids

Eyes: Color: Blue, brown, hazel, green, black.

            Shape: Round, oval, angled

            Special conditions: Very far apart, very close together, bloodshot, watery, cross-

            eyed, missing eye.

Facial: Record color and length of all facial hair, such as beard, goatee, sideburns.

Hair: Mustache: Fu Manchu, handlebar, pencil thin, thick, thin, bushy.

            Beard: Full, goatee, bushy, sparse

Complexion: Light, medium, dark, olive, reddish, freckles, acne, red spots, flaky skin, rash, moles/warts, birthmarks.

PROPERTY

RECORDING THE PROPERTY DESCRIPTION

The property taken should be described in as much detail as possible, giving dimensions, weight, colors, types of materials, and sizes.

Example: 1- Sony compact disk player, serial number 1290887KK, model

IKL, silver exterior, 4" x 4" x 1"   Value $275.00

JEWELRY

Ask the victim for photographs, appraisal documents, or ask them to draw a picture. Include:

Description:	Metal type, color, and kinds (white or yellow, gold, silver)
Stones:	Type, number, kind, color, and size
Mounting:	Type (filigree <ornamental openwork of fine wire>), plain, engraved, etc.
Setting:	Type (basket, Tiffany, box, etc.)
Inscription:	Dates, initials
Style:	Native American, antique, modern, etc.

Example: 1 - 18 carat gold woman's college ring, size 6, "USC" inscribed

on the sapphire stone; initials of "SDS"on the inside   Value $375.00

[**Editor's Note**: All Rolex watches have a model name (e.g., Submariner, Depth Dweller, etc.). This is true of most expensive watches (e.g., Rado, Movado, Breitling, etc.). They also all have serial numbers on the outside and inside of the case. If the victim has a warranty card, it will have the serial number of the watch on it. If the victim has sent in the warranty card to the manufacturer, the company will give you the serial number for that customer.]

FIREARMS

The description should include:

Manufacturer, model number, serial number, caliber or gauge, barrel length, type of finish (stainless steel or blue steel). Also include automatic, semi-automatic, bolt action, slide or pump action, carbine, revolver, derringer, type of grips.

Example: 1 - Smith and Wesson model 19 revolver, 4" barrel, serial number 23988,

blue finish, black rubber grips, loaded with 6 bullets   Value $325.00

RECORDING THE DOLLAR VALUE OF THE LOSS

Note the value based upon the estimate provided by the victim.   Ask for receipts, etc.   If the victim doesn't know, you can generally make an educated guess.   A general rule to follow to estimate value of used property is to estimate what the item would bring at a garage sale.   When the victim has no idea of the value of an item and you can't reasonably come up with a loss amount, consider using various resources to obtain that information.   For instance, a victim has had an antique watch stolen, but the victim has no idea what the watch would be worth.   By calling a local jeweler and describing the item, you would probably be able to come up with an approximate value of the item, which would be better than guessing its value.   Other resources you can use to help you get approximate values on items would be the local telephone directory, which would help in locating appraisers and local dealers that would be able to assist you.

Items that carry no value are blank checks and credit cards.   Until the check is passed or the credit card is actually used to gain cash or other property, there is no loss.   For negotiable items such as cashier's checks, money orders, bonds payable to the bearer, etc., use the face value listed on the item at the time of the theft.   Include the bank name, branch, corporation issuing the bonds, etc., account number, amount and value, dates, names of payee or holder, check number(s), color or design of checks.

For commercial thefts, use the store's replacement cost of the stolen items, not the retail price.

PROPERTY DAMAGE

Do not forget to include the value of property that has been damaged as a result of the criminal act. For example, a car window that has been smashed in an auto burglary is also a loss to the victim, besides the stereo that was taken during the burglary.   Likewise, a house window or door that was pried open or broken during the burglar's entry into the residence is a loss to the victim.   These items should be recorded/listed as damaged property, with a dollar value assigned, and should be mentioned in the narrative. Restitution is being more frequently required as part of a sentence; however, failing to mention these losses could jeopardize restitution being required.

29

VEHICLES

Vehicle thefts are normally reported on special forms used for that purpose and will include blocks entitled:

- Year
- Make
- Body Type
- Model
- Color
- Vehicle Identification Number (VIN)
- License plate number and state

Remember to include:

- Body damage
- Special wheels/rims/tires
- Bumper stickers
- Antennas
- Car phones
- Property inside the vehicle at the time of the theft

DESCRIBING LOCATIONS AND BUILDINGS

It can be very helpful to your reader if he/she knows what type of physical environment (e.g., residential area, commercial district, etc.) the crime occurred in. Crimes such as burglaries and robberies should include a description of the premises and environment. It paints a totally different picture for the reader to learn that a burglary occurred in a 1200 square foot home versus a 6000 square foot home. Likewise, a robbery that occurred in a 1000 square foot convenience store is quite different from a robbery that occurred in a 50,000 square foot warehouse.

When describing locations or buildings, provide as much information as possible. For instance, residences can be described by approximate square footage, number of stories, having an attached garage, alarm system, etc. Provide information about unusual or out-of-the-ordinary circumstances such as a flood control channel or railroad nearby. Such descriptions are best placed at the beginning of the report so the reader can envision the setting.

Example: The victim's residence is a single-story, corner residence, of approximately 1500 square feet and comprises three bedrooms and two baths. The residence has no alarm and is located in a middle-income residential area. Railroad tracks run east/west, approximately 40 feet from and parallel to the six-foot high concrete block wall that runs along the border of the back yards of the houses on the block where the victim's residence is located.

Most businesses tend to be located in commercial or industrial areas. Provide as much information about the specific location (address; major intersection; adjacent businesses; etc.) and the general location, commercial or industrial area; primary industry in the area, if there is one; predominant type of buildings/ structures, if applicable—for example, refinery structures, large warehouses, retail outlets, restaurant area of the business, and a detailed description of it.

Example: The business is located in an industrial area. The business is bordered by a print shop on the north, a delivery service on the south, and an alley to the rear. The building is approximately 15,000 square feet, with a lobby and two offices. Most of the building, about 12,000 square feet, is the warehouse which, at the time of the burglary, contained televisions, stereos, and computers. Only the warehouse has an audible alarm. The alarm is not monitored by a central monitoring station.

COLLECTION OF EVIDENCE

An officer's responsibility in connection with evidence does not stop with locating and booking evidence. Evidence must be identified later in court—perhaps months or years later. The officer must be able to identify the evidence, discuss the circumstances surrounding its finding, and accurately describe what has happened to the evidence since it was first found. This is why each piece of evidence, if it is large enough, should be marked.

Obviously, this requirement is going to make it mandatory to keep some sort of written record for every piece of evidence you locate. You might be called upon to testify as to who found it, where it was found, how many people have handled it and for what purposes. These specific details must be in written form if you are to give acceptable testimony in court. Caution must be used in handling, transporting, and storing evidence. To ensure its value, the evidence must not be altered.

Collecting and processing the evidence is not enough to satisfy the court. The court will want to be assured that the item submitted as evidence is the same item found at the scene. Therefore, the court will want to know exactly what happened to the evidence from the time it was found until it was presented in court. This "history" of the evidence, from the time of its collection to its presentation in court, is called the "chain of custody," and must be documented in writing.

Evidence is handled by many people, including property-room personnel, detectives, and scientific personnel. It is an officer's responsibility to document the chain of custody from the time he/she receives the evidence until it is released from his/her custody. The chain of evidence must include:

1. Who found (discovered, first saw) the item.

2. Where it was found (discovered, first seen).

3. Who recovered (actually, physically picked it up) and marked it, beginning the official custody of the item.

4. Who transported it.

5. Where and when it was booked.

These are issues and concerns that may very well come up in court, so you will need to make sure that your record is complete and accurate.

Narrative

In the narrative of your report, make very clear who actually collected (i.e., picked up and marked, tagged, bagged) and booked each piece of evidence that was, in fact, booked. For example, if you personally, physically collected the evidence, make it clear that you did so. If evidence was collected by someone else at your direction (meaning that you told them to do it), make that just as clear. If evidence was collected and/or booked by someone else and not at your direction, make that clear, too. Just ensure that the reader is able to identify who collected each piece of evidence and who booked each piece of evidence.

Keep in mind that evidence for which a chain of custody cannot be established might be suppressed. If the whereabouts of the evidence and what happened to it cannot be accounted for from the time it was found until it is presented in court, it may be ruled inadmissible.

Examples:	1- man's black leather glove, size 12	Tag #129387
	1- Sears needle-nose pliers with red grips	Tag #292876

24-HOUR CLOCK (00:01 hours to 24:00 hours)

vs.

A.M. / P.M. (12:00 a.m. [midnight] to 11:59 a.m. / 12:00 p.m. [noon] to 11:59 p.m.)

This is one version of the twenty-four hour clock		Standard A.M. / P.M.
24:00 hours, spoken as "twenty-four hundred hours"	=	12:00 a.m. (midnight)
00:01 hours, spoken as "zero zero zero one hours"	=	12:01 a.m. (one minute after midnight)
00:15 hours, spoken as "zero zero fifteen hours"	=	12:15 a.m.
01:00 hours, spoken as "zero one hundred hours"	=	1:00 a.m.
01:05 hours, spoken as "zero one zero five hours"	=	1:05 a.m.
01:15 hours, spoken as "zero one fifteen hours"	=	1:15 a.m.
02:00 hours, spoken as "zero two hundred hours"	=	2:00 a.m.
03:00 hours, spoken as "zero three hundred hours"	=	3:00 a.m.
04:00 hours, spoken as "zero four hundred hours"	=	4:00 a.m.

05:00 hours, spoken as "zero five hundred hours"   =   5:00 a.m.

06:00 hours, spoken as "zero six hundred hours"   =   6:00 a.m.

07:00 hours, spoken as "zero seven hundred hours"   =   7:00 a.m.

08:00 hours, spoken as "zero eight hundred hours"   =   8:00 a.m.

09:00 hours, spoken as "zero nine hundred hours"   =   9:00 a.m.

10:00 hours, spoken as "ten hundred hours"   =   10:00 a.m.

10:15 hours, spoken as "ten fifteen hours"   =   10:15 a.m.

11:00 hours, spoken as "eleven hundred hours"   =   11:00 a.m.

11:15 hours, spoken as "eleven fifteen hours"   =   11:15 a.m.

11:59 hours, spoken as "eleven fifty-nine hours"   =   11:59 a.m. (one minute before noon)

12:00 hours, spoken as "twelve hundred hours"   =   12:00 p.m. (Noon)

13:00 hours, spoken as, "thirteen hundred hours"   =   1:00 p.m.

13:05 hours, spoken as "thirteen zero five hours"   =   1:05 p.m. etc.

13:15 hours, spoken as "thirteen fifteen hours"   =   1:15 p.m.

14:00 hours, spoken as "fourteen hundred hours"   =   2:00 p.m.

15:00 hours, spoken as "fifteen hundred hours"   =   3:00 p.m.

16:00 hours, spoken as "sixteen hundred hours"   =   4:00 p.m.

17:00 hours, spoken as "seventeen hundred hours"   =   5:00 p.m.

18:00 hours, spoken as "eighteen hundred hours"   =   6:00 p.m.

19:00 hours, spoken as "nineteen hundred hours"   =   7:00 p.m.

20:00 hours, spoken as "twenty hundred hours"   =   8:00 p.m.

20:05 hours, spoken as "twenty zero five hours"   =   8:05 p.m.

20:15 hours, spoken as "twenty fifteen hours"   =   8:15 p.m.

21:00 hours, spoken as "twenty-one hundred hours"   =   9:00 p.m.

22:00 hours, spoken as "twenty-two hundred hours"   =   10:00 p.m.

23:00 hours, spoken as "twenty-three hundred hours"   =   11:00 p.m.

23:59 hours, spoken as "twenty-three fifty-nine hours"   =   11:59 p.m. (1 minute before midnight)

24:00 hours, spoken as "twenty-four hundred hours"   =   12:00 a.m. (midnight)

Notes:

CHAPTER 4

PRELIMINARY INVESTIGATIONS

AND

CRIMES THAT JUST OCCURRED

In this chapter you will learn:

- *The 8 components of a preliminary investigation*
- *The information needed for a crime broadcast*

PRELIMINARY INVESTIGATIONS

There are eight components to a Preliminary Investigation. They are:

1) Proceed safely to the scene.

2) Determine the need for emergency medical services, and aid any injured persons.

3) Verify that a crime has occurred. Don't assume the information that was dispatched is a true reflection of events.

4) Identify and arrest the perpetrator(s), if appropriate.

5) As soon as possible, provide dispatch with any suspect information including physical description, direction of flight, loss, mode of travel, weapon, etc.

6) Contain and protect the crime scene and ensure the proper collection of evidence.

7) Locate and interview witnesses and identify other sources of information.

8) Collect all available information necessary to write a clear and accurate report (who, what, where, when, why, and how).

CRIME BROADCAST

Obtain the necessary preliminary information for a crime broadcast. Speed in broadcasting the necessary data is essential. A suspect's vehicle traveling at 30 miles per hour will cover nearly one mile in two minutes. The longer it takes to get information out on the air to nearby police officers, the greater the chance that the suspect(s) will never be caught. As soon as possible, provide dispatch with any information concerning the suspect(s), and his/her method and direction of flight. The following identifying data should be broadcast quickly:

- Type of crime
- Type of business, if applicable
- Location of occurrence
- Time of occurrence
- Number and descriptions of suspects
- Direction the suspect(s) took when leaving the scene
- Whether the suspect(s) traveled on foot or in/on a vehicle
- Description of the vehicle, and weapon, if used
- Description of property taken

As further information is obtained, update the crime broadcast.

Locate, identify, and interview witnesses and other sources of information.

In the case of a crime that just occurred, the interviewing techniques described in Chapter 2 can be too time-consuming. Under this circumstance, it is critical that the first officer on the scene quickly obtain information for a crime broadcast. Information must be obtained promptly if the police officers in the field are to catch a suspect who might still be in the general area, or does not have the time to flee a "safe" distance from the crime scene.

As soon as possible upon arrival at the scene, you should quickly obtain the information needed for a broadcast, such as suspect information, including physical description, direction of flight, mode of travel, weapon, loss/injuries, and specific type of crime.

Once the necessary information is given out over the radio, go back to the person(s) you originally interviewed, and using the Listen, Write, Review method; re-interview them to obtain a complete picture of what occurred. As a result of re-interviewing the parties, you may very well obtain additional information that needs to be added to the crime broadcast.

CHAPTER 5

A REVIEW OF GRAMMAR, PUNCTUATION AND SYNTAX

In this chapter you will review:

- *Grammar- the parts of speech*
- *Syntax- sentence structure / construction*
- *Punctuation*

A well-written report not only includes all the facts, but it also makes sense to the reader and is easy to understand. This requires that sentences be properly structured, the most appropriate words be chosen, and sentences and paragraphs be kept short. In other words, using proper grammar, punctuation, and syntax is essential. These three elements are defined as follows:

GRAMMAR:	The study of language which deals with the form and structure of words (subject, verb, adjective, adverb, etc.—parts of speech)
SYNTAX:	The organization and relationship of word groups, phrases, clauses, and sentences; sentence structure
PUNCTUATION:	A system of using standardized marks in writing and printing to separate sentences or sentence elements or to make the meaning clearer

This chapter serves as a brief review of parts of speech, and common errors that tend to make reports too wordy and hard to understand.

GRAMMAR - PARTS OF SPEECH

<u>Adjective</u>: Modifier that describes nouns.

Examples:

    three guns; *red* hat; *stupid* person

<u>Adverb</u>: Modifier that describes verbs, adjectives, and other adverbs.

Examples:

    ran *quickly*; shot *well*; weather changed *rapidly*

Antecedent: The noun to which a pronoun refers.

Example:

Officer Dobbs shot his gun on Tuesday.

Clause: A group of related words that contains a subject and a predicate. A clause is either independent or dependent. An *independent clause* expresses a complete thought and can stand alone as a sentence. A dependent clause does not express a complete thought and cannot stand alone as a sentence.

Example:

She will work in homicide investigation   (*dependent clause*) when she is transferred (*independent clause*).

Conjunction: Connecting word.

Examples:

   and, or, but, neither, nor, for, yet, so

Interjection: Expresses exclamation.

Examples:

   Police! Fire! Stop!

Modifier: Word, clause, or phrase that describes or explains another word.   Adverbs (describe verbs, adjectives or other adverbs) and adjectives (describe nouns or pronouns) are examples of modifiers.

Examples:

   adjectives: *three* suspects ran; a *screaming* victim died; a *blue* van arrived

   adverbs: she shot *quickly*; she strangled him *slowly*; she writes *well*

Noun: A word which names a person, place, thing/object, or idea.

Examples:

   gun, computer, Officer Jones, fireman, office

Object: Follows and receives the action of the verb.

Examples:

> Officer Jones shot the gun.
>
> Officer Jones arrested the suspect.

Preposition: A word that shows relationship.

Examples:

> to, at, by, for, on, between, below, above

Pronoun: A word that takes the place of a noun, in many cases so that the noun doesn't have to be repeated.   A pronoun, like a noun, can be the subject (nominative case: I, you, he, they, we), object (objective case: her, him, me, them, us), or show possession (possessive case: mine, hers, yours)

Example:

Officer Jones finished his report and handed *it* to *her*.

Examples:

> I, you, he, she, it, me, you, they, us, we, them, my, mine, your, yours, their.

Sentence: A group of words comprised of a subject and a verb that states a complete thought.

Example:

Mr. Smith was the victim of the crime.

Subject: Expresses the person speaking, the person spoken to, the person or thing spoken about; a fundamental element in a sentence. It tells the reader who or what is performing the action in a sentence.

Examples:

The *crime scene investigator* examined the gun.

Officer Jones arrested the suspect.

Verb: Any word that shows or depicts action in a sentence.

Examples: shoots, am, is, examines, ran

> The crime scene investigator *examined* the gun.

> Officer Jones *arrested* the suspect.

> The suspect *ran* down the alley.

> The suspect *shot* the victim.

> The victim *is* bleeding.

Lie / Lay (not the "lie" that refers to a false statement—this section refers to the verb)

[Probably the major reason lie and lay are confusing is their past tenses, and most troublesome of all is the use of "lay" as the past tense of "lie."]

	Intransitive	Transitive
Present Tense:	Lie, Lies	Lay, Lays
Past Tense:	Lay	Laid
Past Participle:	Lain	Laid
Present Participle:	Lying	Laying

An intransitive verb takes no direct object. It does not act on anyone or anything else.

A transitive verb takes a direct object. It is something you do to someone or something else. It acts on someone or something else.

"Lie" is an intransitive verb (it takes no direct object). It does not act on anyone or anything else.

"Lie": *to be in a reclining position along a relatively horizontal surface.*

"To Lie": *to recline; to put oneself in a reclining position along a relatively horizontal surface.*

Remember—the past tense of lie is lay.

Examples:

Present Tense (lie, lies):

1) Lie on the grass until the paramedics get here.

2) The suspect told the victim to lie down and be quiet.

3) Lie down and go to sleep.

Past Tense (lay):

1) The victim lay there until the paramedics arrived.

2) The suspect lay in wait for 3 hours until the victim finally got home.

Present Participle (lying)

1) We found the gun lying on the covered ledge, where the suspect said he left it.

Past Participle (lain)

1) We found the gun on the ledge, where it had lain since the suspect left it there 20 years ago.
1) If the suspect had not confessed, the body could have lain in the cave forever and never been found.

NOTE: Proper use of the past tense may seem awkward at first, but you have to get used to it.

"Lay" is a <u>transitive</u> verb (it takes a direct object).   It acts upon someone or something else. "Lay":

to place or put so as to be in a resting or reclining position; to deposit.

Remember —the past tense of <u>lay</u> is <u>laid</u>

Examples:

Present Tense (lay, lays)

1) Lay the gun on the ground.
2) Watch the suspect closely as she lays the bomb on the ground and steps back.
3) I like to lay my head on a pillow when I sleep.

Past Tense (laid)

    1) I laid the evidence bag on the counter so the clerk could pick it up and store it.
    2) She laid the gun on the table when I told her to, and then she stepped away.

Present Participle (laying)

    1) I like laying the facts out chronologically when possible so the report is easier to follow.

Past Participle (laid)

    1) The suspects have laid a trail of misleading evidence.

Notes:

SYNTAX - Sentence Structure / Construction

Syntax is the way to construct phrases, clauses and sentences. Readability studies show that sentences of fewer than 20 words are best for comprehension, with an average sentence consisting of 15-17 words. When you write, keep sentences simple, with one primary thought per sentence.

Sentence Fragment

Too often, officers tend to write the way they think, and the result is an *incomplete sentence* or a *sentence fragment*. An incomplete sentence, also called a sentence fragment, may contain a subject and a verb but does not express a complete thought.

Example: The car is on the east side of the street. At the edge of a milepost.

Should be:

The car is on the east side of the street, at the edge of a milepost.

Run-on Sentence

A run-on sentence results from completely omitting punctuation between two or more sentences.

Example:

As I passed the store I saw a man staggering eastbound on 10th Street he stumbled twice and fell to the ground.

Should be:

As I passed the store, I saw a man staggering eastbound on 10th Street. He stumbled twice and fell to the ground.

Misplaced Modifier

A misplaced modifier appears to modify a word other than the one it was intended to modify (usually because the modifier was put in the wrong place in the sentence).

Example:

An evidence tag was found in the courtroom that was thought to be lost. (The courtroom isn't lost, is it?)

Should be:

An evidence tag that was thought to be lost was found in the courtroom.

Or

The lost evidence tag was found in the courtroom.

Example:

I thought the chief accidentally dropped the report I had been drafting in the trash can.   (I wasn't drafting the report in the trash can.)

Should be:

I couldn't find the report I had been drafting. I thought the chief accidentally dropped it into the trash can.

Example:

Here are some suggestions for protecting your valuables from our burglary investigators while on vacation. (What? Who's on vacation? Are the valuables going to be protected from the investigators?)

Should be:

Here are some helpful suggestions from our burglary investigators for protecting your valuables while you are on vacation.

The difference between "Recognize" and Identify"

Two words that officers tend to use incorrectly are identify and recognize.   Although many people may interchange them while using them in speech, misuse can cause confusion in a report.

Recognize: To make out as or perceive to be something previously known. This means you've seen it/him/her before.

Identify: To establish the identity of; show or prove the sameness of (as with something known, stated, possessed).   This means you have not seen it/him/her before, but perhaps read or heard a description of it/him/her.

To recognize implies a prior knowledge or experience of or with the person, place, thing, or sensation you are talking about.   You can't "recognize" or recall someone or something without previously having seen or interacted with the person, been to the particular place, experienced the particular sensation, touched the particular object, etc.

To identify someone or something means that you compare that person, place or thing to a standard, to a definition, or to a description. Depending on how similar the person, place, or thing is to the standard or definition or description, you can say that his, her, or its identity has been established. You have shown or proved the sameness of the person, place, or thing with the standard, definition, or description.

Pronouns with Multiple Nouns

If two nouns are joined by *and*, the pronoun is usually plural.

Example:

    Officer Smith and Officer Jones brought their reports to the briefing.

If both male and female are involved, it's better to change the wording from singular to plural.

Examples:

    Instead of: Each sergeant must meet with his or her staff.

    Use: Sergeants must meet with their staffs

When a pronoun refers to nouns joined by *or, nor, either… or*, or *neither … nor*, and one of the nouns is plural, make the pronoun match the closest noun.

Example:

    Neither Joe nor the Browns drove their cars.

Double Negative

Examples:

    The suspect vehicle was not unlike a jeep in appearance.

    I didn't not complete the report; I just didn't fill in all the boxes on the face sheet.

Don't use double negatives; just write:

    "The suspect vehicle looked like a jeep."   "The suspect vehicle resembled a jeep."

    "I completed the report except for the three boxes I left blank."

Some of the most common syntax errors involve *agreement,* and *who vs. whom.*

Agreement means that the use of some words in a sentence requires the specific use of other words. The errors that are most often seen in reports tend to be errors in subject-verb agreement and noun-pronoun agreement.

A. Subject - Verb Agreement

The subject and verb must agree in number. A singular subject needs a singular verb; a plural subject needs a plural verb.

Examples:

We (subject) are (verb) the best officers in the department.   (Plural)

I (subject) am (verb) planning to go to the range to shoot. (Singular)

To assist you in identifying whether you need a singular or plural verb, ignore phrases and clauses that separate the subject from the verb.

Examples:

The gun (subject, singular) containing the shell casings was (verb, singular) a revolver.

Security officers (subject, plural), along with the firemen, have (verb, plural) to put out the fire.

A writer will often, mistakenly, make the verb agree with the word that comes before it instead of agreeing with the subject of the sentence.

Incorrect: The Police Commission's members, one of whom is a banker, votes tonight.

Correct: The Police Commission's members, one of whom is a banker, vote tonight.

The writer made *votes* agree with the last word that came into his or her mind (*banker*) instead of with the word it should agree with (*members*).

Incorrect: Only one of the guns are missing.

Correct: Only one of the guns is missing.

Incorrect: Few members of the gang is still alive.

Correct: Few members of the gang are still alive.

When two or more subjects are joined by *and*, use a plural verb. When two or more singular subjects are joined by *or* or *nor*, use a singular verb. If the subjects are of different numbers, make the verb agree with the subject nearest the verb.

Examples:

Officers Jones and Smith (subject, plural) have been working (verb, plural) on the case all week.

Either a citation or a report (subject, singular) is (verb, singular) to be written before the end of the day.

Use a singular verb after: *each, every, everyone, everybody, nobody, someone, everyone, another* and *much.*

Examples:

Every officer is on duty.

Everybody was present for the swearing in.

Use a plural verb after *both, few many, others*, and *several.*

Examples:

Both guns are out of ammunition.

Many were asked, but few were able to answer.

Collective Nouns:

If the group is acting as one unit, use a singular verb.

Examples:

The Police Board of Directors meets on Tuesdays.

The pistol team is one of the best in the area.

If the members of the group are acting separately, use a plural verb.

Example:

The Safety Committee members are not in agreement on the decision.

B. Noun - Pronoun Agreement

The general rule is that a noun and its pronoun must agree, in person and in number, whether they act as subject, object, or possessor.

Examples:

I must stand by my trainee, just as you must stand by yours.

Jack said he shot the gun.

June likes her patrol assignment.

The department won't change its policy.

Proper usage of Who and Whom and their derivatives.

Use *who* and *whoever* when you can substitute *he, she, I* or *we* for the "who" clause.

Examples:

Who was promoted to sergeant?

Who did they say was chosen to fill in?

Use *whom* and *whomever* when you can substitute *him, her, them, me* or *us* as the object of the verb or the object of the preposition in the "whom" clause.

Examples:

She will speak to whomever answers the question.

Write to whomever you think can supply the information quickly.

Another approach is to look at the word that comes after your choice of *who* or *whom* in the sentence. If that word is a verb or an adverb, your choice <u>almost always</u> will be <u>who</u>. If the word that comes after your choice of *who* or *whom* is not a verb or an adverb, your choice will almost always be *whom*.

Example:

Who/Whom wants to transport the suspect to the station?

Since the word *wants*, which comes after your choice of who/whom, is a verb, chances are the word you want is *who*.

Who wants to transport the suspect to the station?

Example:

Officer Jones, who/whom Chief Smith is considering promoting, won the award this year.

Since the word Chief, which comes after your choice of who/whom, is not a verb or an adverb, your choice would be *whom.*

Officer Jones, whom <u>Chief</u> Smith is considering promoting, won the award this year.

PUNCTUATION

A good general rule to follow with punctuation is to always have a reason for what you do. When in doubt, leave it out!

There are more than 30 punctuation marks, but in police report writing only 10 or 12 of them should be used.

The Period   (.)

The period means to "Stop." Use it often, because it helps to keep sentences short and eliminates problems that come from constructing longer, confusing sentences.

Periods are used:

    1) to end sentences

    2) in abbreviations (8 a.m., U.S.A., Off. S. Brown). However, many abbreviations no longer contain periods, especially abbreviations of names of agencies, corporations, and colleges (CIA, IBM, USC).

    3) after numerals or letters preceding listed items

    4) with decimals

<u>Don't</u> use periods:

    1)   in acronyms

    2)   after displayed headings

    3)   after listed items that aren't complete sentences

The Colon (:)

The colon is used to:

1) Introduce something that explains or illustrates what has come before it.

Example:

>   This is the mission of our special patrol: to fight crime.

2) Introduce a list or a series of examples.

Example:

>   There are three steps to writing a good report: plan, write, and correct.

The Comma (,)

1) Use a comma to separate items in a series of three or more.

Examples:

>   The witness said he saw the burglar steal a gun, a knife, and the cash register.
>
>   The suspect kicked in the door, shot the victim, and fled on foot.

2) Use a comma when something comes before the subject of the sentence.

Examples:

>   No, he can't come to court.
>
>   When the witness came to court, she got lost.
>
>   When she saw the traffic collision, the officer stopped and provided medical aid to the driver.

3) When you combine two or more sentences and connect them with FOR, AND, NOR, BUT, OR, YET, or SO, use a comma before the connecting word.   These connecting words are arranged to spell out *FANBOYS* to help you remember the punctuation rule.

Examples:

He reached for his baton. He caught his foot on the carpeting

Combined: He reached for his baton, but he caught his foot on the carpeting.

Jones was lying. He got caught.

Combined: Jones was lying, and he got caught.

4) When you interrupt the flow of the sentence to add information, you may surround that interrupting information with commas.

Example:

He said that he had, in fact, fired the gun that killed the victim.

The Semi-colon (;)

Since the semi-colon is used in much the same way as the period. It is often used as a crutch to minimize run-on sentences in a police report.

The Apostrophe (')

The apostrophe has two major uses:

1) The apostrophe takes the place of missing letters in contractions.

Examples:

It's a gun.

You shouldn't arrest him.

It wouldn't be right to take him to jail.

Note: *It's* is a contraction for *it is*. *It's time to leave.* (It is time to leave.)

It's is also a contraction for *it has*. *It's been raining all day.* (It has been raining all day.) *It's* is

never used to show the possessive case of "it."

The possessive case of *it* is written *its*. (*The car rolled over and came to rest on its roof.*)

2) The apostrophe indicates possession.

Examples:

The officer's gun was damaged. (Referring to one officer and one gun)

The officers' guns were damaged. (Referring to multiple officers and guns) The

boss's car is dirty. (Referring to one boss)

The bosses' cars are dirty. (Referring to more than one boss and more than one car)

When the possessive word is singular, the apostrophe comes before the *s*. When the possessive word is plural, the apostrophe comes after the *s*.

An exception is people's names ending in *s*. With some names, we add an *'s* and with others we just add an apostrophe.

Examples:

Charles's gun is dirty.

We drove to Officer Jones' house.

We generally add an *'s* to first names ending in *s* and add only an apostrophe to last names ending in *s*. A clue for choosing correctly is sound. When speaking the person's name, if we add the *s* after the apostrophe, then we also add the *s* when we write that person's name. If we don't add the *s* when we speak, we leave it out when we write and just add the apostrophe.

The apostrophe also shows possession for pairs of nouns. The rule is to use *'s* after the second noun.

Examples:

John and Walt's gun...

The sergeant and victim's statements...

If your intention is to show individual possession rather than joint possession, use an *s* after both nouns:

Example:

John's and Walt's guns.

Quotation Marks ("   "), ('   ')

1) <u>Double quotation marks are used, in pairs, to:</u>

   a) Identify or indicate (enclose) direct quotations short enough to run into the text (quotations of more than three or four lines usually appear without quotation marks but are set off from the text by space, indentation, etc.). When you quote, you quote the exact words of the victim, witness, suspect, etc.

Example:

Roberta Smith said, "I shot him."

[Note that you have chosen to quote Smith because you want to use her statement, the exact words. In the example above, you use Smith's words, and since Smith uses "I" to express herself, you should use "I" as well.]

b) Identify or indicate words or phrases which follow or are introduced by such words or expressions as *signed, entitled, marked, and labeled.*

Example:

The exhibit was labeled "Murder Weapon."

2) <u>Single quotation marks are used, in pairs, to enclose a quotation within another quotation.</u>
Example:

Officer Smith said, "Put the gun in the locker marked 'Danger'."

Example:

The victim said, "After the robber hit me with the gun, he said 'If you say anything, I'll shoot you,' so I kept my mouth shut."

3) <u>Indirect quotes do not require quotation marks.</u>

Example:

Smith said that she shot him.

4) <u>Where to put them:</u>

- Periods and commas always go inside the closing quotation mark. This is the common practice in the United States, the preferred American style. Since you're writing your reports in the U.S., use the U.S. practice.

- Colons and semicolons always go outside the quotation marks. Question marks and exclamation points go either inside or outside of the quotation marks, depending on whether they are part of the quotation.

5) <u>As a general rule:</u>
- Place periods and commas inside the quotation marks.
- Place colons and semicolons outside the quotation marks.

The Dash (—)

The dash most often serves in place of a comma, semicolon, colon or parentheses. In police report writing avoid using the dash.

The Slash (\ )

The slash can mean "and", "or", "either one", and "both". It is best to not use the slash because it can be confusing to the reader.

Parentheses (( ))

Parentheses, like commas and dashes, can be used to add information to a sentence. Parentheses slow the reader down and indicate that the information enclosed in the parentheses is optional.

Parentheses can be used to:

1) refer to something or someone;

Example:

    Officer Jones referred to his report (page 34) for additional information.

2) enclose the abbreviations or acronyms of spelled-out forms, or vice versa;

Example:

    The Federal Bureau of Investigation (FBI) offered their help.

3) indicate the source of information or explanation within the text;

Example:

    Recent studies on crime (Wilson, 1993) show that crime is on the decrease for most age groups.

The Hyphen (-)

1)   A hyphen connects compound nouns.

Example:

    My father-in-law is late.

2)   A hyphen connects compound verbs.

Example:

    You should double-space that report.

3)   A hyphen connects compound adjectives.

Example:

His report is on twentieth-century law enforcement.

Not all compound words are hyphenated.   Sometimes a compound word will require a hyphen and sometimes it won't.   It can depend how the word is used in a sentence.   *Use common sense and a dictionary when in doubt.*

4)   A hyphen can divide a word of more than two syllables at the end of a line.

Example:

When an officer is preparing to testify on a case, he will go to the department and obtain a copy of the police report.

5)   To maintain a professional appearance to the report:

    ·   Avoid ending more than two consecutive lines with hyphens.

    ·   Avoid ending the first and last lines of paragraphs with hyphens.

    ·   Avoid dividing a line-ending word after only one syllable. Put the whole word on the next line.

    ·   Avoid hyphenating the last word on a page; move the whole word to the next page.

Notes:

CHAPTER 6

SLANG, JARGON, ACRONYMS, INITIALS & ABBREVIATIONS

In this chapter you will learn:

- *The proper use of slang*
- *The proper use of jargon*
- *The proper use of acronyms*
- *The acceptable abbreviations of words*

In most professions, slang and jargon are commonly used, law enforcement and security are no different. It is important to keep in mind that such language, in most cases, is inappropriate for report writing. Not only does it sound bad, it is not easily understood and can be misinterpreted; where the reader lives or works can influence his or her interpretation of slang, jargon, and acronyms. Only when quoting someone should slang and/or jargon be included, and then the officer should always confirm the meaning with the person being quoted so there is no mistake as to what was meant.

SLANG

SLANG is defined as inappropriate "street" language. Many times a slang word is a perfectly acceptable and commonly used word in everyday English but has a new meaning attached to it.

Examples:

Slang term

Split   - To run away from

Heavy hitter   - An important or powerful person (for example, in a career, field, crime hierarchy, business, etc.)

Freak / Freak out - Meaning, to react with extreme or irrational distress

Hip   - Sophisticated, knowing, aware

Phat   - Very good, excellent

JARGON

JARGON is defined as the specialized vocabulary and idioms of those in the same work, way of life, etc., now usually called "shoptalk."

Examples:

Jargon		Meaning
Paper hanger	-	Writer of bad checks
Deuce	-	Person under the influence of alcohol while driving
Flake	-	Irresponsible person
Cat burglar	-	Person who burglarizes at night while people are at home

When quoting the slang and jargon of victims, witnesses and suspects, ALWAYS clarify with the speaker what is meant by the word or phrase. You <u>may</u> understand what the person says but that doesn't mean that the reader will. As you can see by the examples above, any of these words and phrases can have multiple interpretations.

ACRONYMS AND INITIALS

ACRONYM: a word formed from the first or first few letters of a series of words. Acronyms are frequently used in both writing and speaking, but <u>can</u> be confusing. No matter how sure you are that everybody knows what the letters mean, unless the acronym is one which has, through usage, practically come to be used as a word in its own right, such as radar, sonar, scuba, laser, etc., use the full name, in all capitals, with no periods. Those readers who do know what it means won't be offended, and those who don't know will appreciate it. An acronym replaces a series of words and is pronounced like a word.

Examples of acronyms:

Laser	Light amplification by stimulated emission of radiation
Radar	Radio detecting and ranging
AIDS	Acquired Immune Deficiency Syndrome
CONUS	Continental United States
Sonar	Sound navigation and ranging
NOW	National Organization for Women
PIN	Personal Identification Number

ZIP (code)   Zone Improvement Plan

Scuba   self contained underwater breathing apparatus

INITIALS: Some well-known organizations, objects, phrases, etc. are more frequently referred to by their initials (i.e., the first letter of each word of the name) than by their full name. These are written in all-capital abbreviation form, with no periods. They are pronounced letter-by-letter. They are not acronyms. For example:

IRS	Internal Revenue Service
ICE	United States Immigration and Customs Enforcement
TSA	Transportation Security Administration
DHS	United States Department of Homeland Security
CHP	California Highway Patrol
FBI	Federal Bureau of Investigation
CIA	Central Intelligence Agency
DOJ	Department of Justice
LAPD	Los Angeles Police Department / Los Alamitos Police Department
ATF	(Bureau of) Alcohol, Tobacco, and Firearms
HUD	United States Department of Housing and Urban Development
OSHA	Occupational Safety and Health Administration
NASA	National Aeronautics and Space Administration
NIMBY	Not In My Back Yard

If the name is going to be used several times in a report, consider doing this: the first time you use the term write "National Aeronautics and Space Administration (NASA)," and then use "NASA" for all repeat uses. For a single use, it is best to write out the entire name, however bothersome it may seem.

ABBREVIATIONS

An ABBREVIATION is a shortened form of a word or phrase.

Examples of abbreviations:

"Blvd." for Boulevard

"lb." for pound

"St." for street

"Ave." for Avenue

Abbreviations are acceptable in report writing as long as the abbreviation is commonly used and understood by the average person. Words that can be abbreviated will save you time when writing your report especially if they are frequently used. However, too often, officers make up their own abbreviations, not realizing that the reader may not understand the meaning.

Abbreviations should only be used sparingly, when space is limited, or when the same word is used repeatedly in the report narrative. Be consistent within the same material; do not abbreviate a term in some sentences and spell it out in other sentences. Use the same abbreviation throughout the report. Unnecessary and frequent use of acronyms and abbreviations makes an officer look lazy. When using an abbreviation or acronym that may not be commonly understood, write the entire word(s) out first, followed by the abbreviation or acronym in parentheses. This allows the abbreviation or acronym to be understood throughout the report instead of continually referring to the entire word(s).

NOTE: A good rule to follow with acronyms and abbreviations is "If in doubt, write it out!"

The following is a list of commonly recognized, standard abbreviations which can be used in report writing:

Months	Abbreviation
January	Jan.
February	Feb.
March	Mar.
April	Apr.
May	May
June	Jun.
July	Jul.
August	Aug.
September	Sept.
October	Oct.
November	Nov.
December	Dec.

Days of the Week	Abbreviation
Monday	Mon.
Tuesday	Tues.
Wednesday	Wed.
Thursday	Thurs.
Friday	Fri.
Saturday	Sat.
Sunday	Sun.

Time	Abbreviation
second, seconds	sec., secs.
minute, minutes	min., mins.
hour, hours	hr., hrs.
week, weeks	wk., wks.
month, months	mo., mos.
year, years	yr., yrs.

Measurements	Abbreviation
Amount	Amt.
Dozen	Doz.
Inch	In.
Feet (&foot)	Ft.
Gram	Gr.
Height	Hgt.
Kilogram	Kg.
Kilometer	Km.
Length	L.
Measurement	Meas.
Mile	Mi.
Ounce	Oz.
Pound	Lb.
Pounds	Lbs.
Weight	Wt.
Width	W.
Yard	Yd.

Term	Abbreviation
Administration	Admin.
Approximate	Approx.
Bureau	Bur.
Assistant	Asst.
Attorney	Atty.
Attempt	Att.
Building	Bldg.
Captain	Capt.
Driver's License	DL.
Company	Co.
Court	Ct.
Date of Birth	DOB
Dead on Arrival	DOA
Defendant	Def.
Department	Dept.
Degree	Deg.
Detective	Det.
Department of Motor Vehicles	DMV.
Director	Dir.
Division	Div.
District	Dist.
Doctor	Dr.
Doing Business As	DBA
Driving Under the Influence	DUI

Term	Abbreviation
Eastbound	E/B
Example	Ex.
Federal	Fed.
Gauge	Ga.
Government	Govt.
Headquarters	Hqt.
Highway	Hwy
Hospital	Hosp.
Identification	ID
Informant	Inf.
Inspector	Insp.
Junction	Junc.
Junior	Jr.
Juvenile	Juv.
Last Known Address	LKA
License	Lic.
Lieutenant	Lt.
Maximum	Max.
Medium	Med.
Memorandum	Memo.
Misdemeanor	Misd.
Not Applicable	N/A
Northbound	N/B
Number	No.
Numbers	Nos.
Officer	Ofc.
Organization	Org.
Passenger	Pass.
Permanent / Personal Identification Number	PIN
Place	Pl.
Point of Entry	POE
Point of Impact	POI
Point of Rest	POR
Police Officer / Probation Officer	PO
Quantity	Qty.
Quart	Qt.
Reporting Party	R/P
Road	Rd.
Railroad	RR
School	Sch.
Section	Sect.

Term	Abbreviation
Serial	Ser.
Sergeant	Sgt.
Southbound	S/B
Subject	Subj.
Suspect	Susp.
Unable to Locate	UTL
Unknown	Unk.
Vehicle Identification Number	VIN
Victim	Vict. or V/.
Witness	Wit. or W/.

SUSPECT ABBREVIATIONS

When listing abbreviations which include race, gender and age, list them in that order:

Examples:

    I.   White female adult (WFA)

    II.   Black male juvenile (BMJ)

    III.   Hispanic male adult (HMA)

Notes:

CHAPTER 7

WRITING THE REPORT

In this chapter you will learn about:

- *Active voice*
- *First person*
- *Past tense*
- *Block printing*
- *Paraphrasing vs. quoting*
- *Big words vs. small words*
- *Specific vs. vague words*
- *Homonyms*
- *Word choice*
- *Wordy expressions*
- *Redundant expressions*
- *Double negatives*
- *Avoiding sexist and biased language*
- *Lengthy reports*
- *Conclusionary writing*

_____

Now that you've interviewed everyone involved in an incident and have taken adequate notes, you must write the report. At the end of this Manual (Appendix S) is a variety of sample reports that can help guide you.

In most instances, you should write the report the way the event actually occurred. That is, typically, you arrive at the scene and talk to the victim of the crime first because you need to establish that a crime occurred. Most of the time, the victim will be the best source of information. After you have talked to the victim (s), you talk to the witness (es). You may talk to the suspect next, and finalize the report with additional investigation that you do or assign to someone else. Writing the report in this order makes it easy for the reader to follow and to understand. Keep in mind that one of the purposes of a report is to fully inform the reader of what occurred by presenting, in a concise, organized format, all the relevant facts. Try to paint a word-picture of the incident with your goal to put the reader at the scene of the event.

Since writing is thinking, the adequacy of a report is dependent not only on the technical writing skills of the officer, but also on the officer's ability to accurately and completely understand all relevant aspects of the incident. Only after the incident is completely understood and all relevant information gathered and evaluated can a written record of the incident be produced. Never assume the reader will know what you mean if you haven't written what you mean!

_____

ACTIVE VOICE

Writing reports using the active voice leaves no doubt in the reader's mind as to who did what. Active voice makes the sentence easier to understand and often makes the sentence shorter. Passive voice is weak and imprecise and leaves important questions unanswered. Using the active voice reduces writing by at least 20% because it is direct and to the point. You eliminate unnecessary words.

Example:

    The car was driven onto the freeway. (Passive)

Naturally, you would ask 'Who drove the car onto the freeway?'

The sentence should be rewritten to say 'I drove the car onto the freeway.' (Active)

The easiest way to write an active voice sentence is to put the doer (noun) at the very beginning of the sentence and in front of the action (verb).

Example:

    Instead of writing: 'The fingerprint was found on the table',

        Write: 'Officer Smith found the fingerprint on the table.'

    Instead of writing   'The gun was fired.'

        Write 'I fired the gun.'

FIRST PERSON

Write using the first person form "I," "we," or "my partner and I." First person is easier to understand, more natural and direct. Writing in the third person can be more complex.

Do not refer to yourself as "the reporting officer" or "the writer of this report." When you wish to refer to yourself, write "I" or when referring to both you and your partner* simply write "we". Your report must clearly state who is reporting.

As a grammar term, "person" refers to:

    1)   First person, the <u>speaker</u> or <u>writer</u>: I, we, Officer Smith and I;

    2)   Second person, the person spoken <u>to</u>: you;

    3)   Third person, the person spoken <u>about</u>: she, they, the victim, Smith.

63

For example, to say, "This officer verbally advised Smith to give this officer the mace belonging to this officer" is written in third person. The sentence would make better sense and be less wordy if it was rewritten as "I told Smith to give my mace back to me."

Likewise, to say, "I, Officer Smith, drove the suspect to jail" is written in third person. It should be rewritten to simply say, "I drove the suspect to jail."

[*Note: it is unwise to put your name and your partner's name as the reporting officers on the bottom of any report. List all officers present during the investigation. Even if an officer doesn't do anything (he just stands by and listens) he should be listed as a witness. If you wrote the report, only your name should be listed as the reporting officer. If your partner was present during interviews, etc., you should explain in your narrative what input your partner provided. If necessary, the partner officer should be listed as a witness, or better yet, he/she should write a supplemental report to your report.*]

PAST TENSE

When writing the report, write in past tense. Most of what people will tell you is about an incident or series of events that already occurred. The events are not occurring as you write the report, nor are they likely to occur in the future. For instance, a victim of a crime may tell you, "I see this guy break into my neighbor's house." You would write, "The witness told me that she saw someone break into her neighbor's house."

EXCEPTIONS:

There are exceptions to always writing in past tense. For example, if the victim wants to prosecute the suspect, you can't very well write, "The victim wanted to prosecute the suspect" because it would leave your reader with the impression that the victim was willing to prosecute at one time but now is not willing to do so. You should write, "The victim is willing to prosecute."

Another example might be, "The victim will call the police station when she completes the inventory list of her losses." You can't write that she had called because that would leave the reader with the impression that the victim already called the police department about the list when she has not yet done so.

The following is a list of present and past tenses of the more common verbs used in report writing. The present tense is followed by the past tense:

Arise / Arose	Become / Became	Bleed / Bled
Be / Was	Begin / Began	Blow / Blew
Beat / Beat	Bite / Bit	Break / Broke

Bring / Brought	Fly / Flew	Pay / Paid
Build / Built	Forget / Forgot	Put /Put
Burst / Burst	Freeze / Froze	Quit / Quit
Buy / Bought	Get / Got	Read / Read
Can / Could	Give / Gave	Ride / Rode
Catch /Caught	Go / Went	Ring / Rang
Choose / Chose	Grow / Grew	Run / Ran
Cling / Clung	Hang / Hung	Say / Said
Come / Came	Have / Had	See / Saw
Cost / Cost	Hear / Heard	Seek / Sought
Cut / Cut	Hide / Hid	Sell / Sold
Deal / Dealt	Hit / Hit	Send / Sent
Die / Died	Hold / Held	Shake / Shook
Dig / Dug	Hurt / Hurt	Shine / Shone
Do / Did	Is / Was / Were	Shoot / Shot
Draw / Drew	Keep / Kept	Show / Showed
Drink / Drank	Kill / Killed	Shut / Shut
Drive / Drove	Know / Knew	Shrink / Shrank
Eat / Ate	Lay / Laid	Sing / Sang
Fall / Fell	Lead / Led	Sink / Sank
Feed / Fed	Leave / Left	Sit / Sat
Feel / Felt	Let / Let	Sleep / Slept
Fit / Fit	Lie / Lay	Speak / Spoke
Flee / Fled	Lose / Lost	Speed / Sped
Fight / Fought	Make / Made	Spend / Spent
Find / Found	Meet / Met	Spring / Sprang

Stab/Stabbed	Teach / Taught	Wear / Wore
Stand/Stood	Tear / Tore	Weave / Wove
Steal/Stole	Tell / Told	Win / Won
Strike / Struck	Think / Thought	Write / Wrote
Swear / Swore	Throw / Threw	
Swing / Swung	Try / Tried	
Swim / Swam	Understand / Understood	
Take / Took	Wake / Woke	

BLOCK PRINTING

Most organizations are in the process of implementing computerized reports; however, departments still require officers have the ability to write the report by hand. If your organization uses computers to write reports, make sure that you review Chapter 8, Report Writing Responsibilities for Supervisors, which discusses some of the problems encountered when officers use computers to prepare reports.

When hand printing, block printing is most commonly used. Block printing refers to printing by using all capital letters. Lower case is not used. When using block printing, all letters and numbers are the same size. A writing template or ruler can be used to write in all block letters. Block printing makes the report look neat and uniform, but can be very difficult to read.

THIS SENTENCE IS A FORM OF BLOCK PRINTING.

WRITING STYLES: CATEGORY & NARRATIVE

There are essentially two types of report writing styles used today: Category and Narrative. The first style, Category, is written with a topic or heading at the top of the page.

After you have provided a brief description of loss, injuries, or any other vital information, state how you received the call. To begin that part of the report, you might title it Source or Information. Under this heading, you would tell the reader how you received the call, what time you arrived, and what you saw when you arrived.

The next heading might be entitled Victim Statement because in most instances the first person you talk to will be the victim. Under this heading, state what the victim told you.

The next heading might be entitled <u>Witness Statement</u> because in most instances the second person you talk to is the witness. Under this heading, state what the witness told you.

If a suspect is located and you interview him/her, you would entitle your next heading as <u>Suspect Statement</u> and under this heading, state what the suspect told you.

The next part of the investigation will usually include your narrative telling the reader what you did. You might title it "<u>Officer's Actions</u>" or "<u>Investigation</u>." Under this heading you might inspect a residence for signs of entry, discover evidence or property, arrest the suspect, etc. You would describe in detail what you did to bring the investigation to a satisfactory conclusion.

The last heading is usually entitled "<u>Disposition</u>." Under this heading you tell the reader the status of the case; you transported and booked the suspect and on what charges, you left the scene in the care of the crime scene investigator, you referred the case to the investigators, etc.

The second method of writing is called Narrative. The same information is provided in the same order as discussed above using the Category style of writing, except the headings are not used.

PARAPHRASING vs. QUOTING

<u>Victims and Witnesses</u>

Paraphrasing is defined as "the rewording of the meaning expressed in something spoken or written." Much of what victims and witnesses tell you can be paraphrased. You take the statements they give to you and put the statements in your own language. This eliminates unnecessary information that they gave you, but conveys the same information.

Example:

> A victim, Mr. Jones, tells you, "I went to the AM/PM store about 9:00 a.m. today to get some soap and toilet paper and came home about 2:00 p.m. to find that the house had been broken into. I know that I locked everything up and I know that they stole my TV set. I don't know what the world is coming to these days."

You would paraphrase or rewrite it this way:

> Mr. Jones told me that he had left this morning at about 9 a.m. He said that the house was locked up. He returned about 2 p.m. today to discover the house had been broken into and a TV had been stolen.

In the above example, the victim's statements have been paraphrased, which has reduced the wording by one third but retained the essential information. In most instances, there is no reason to quote victims or witnesses. The exception to this is with statements that a victim may make, especially when the statement shows obvious fear. Statements such as these tend to be powerful during trial.

For instance, a victim of an armed robbery tells you, "I knew that he knew I saw him because I looked him in the face. I knew he would have to kill me."

You could paraphrase this statement, but in doing so, the statement would have less impact. It should be quoted exactly as given by the victim.

Suspects' Statements

In general, paraphrase statements of suspects. Quote <u>exact</u> statements that tend to:

- Show knowledge of the crime
- Show inconsistencies in statements
- Be admissions or confessions to a criminal act
- Show remorse or lack of remorse, anger
- Show motive, intent

If you are in doubt as to whether you should quote or paraphrase a suspect's statement, go ahead and quote it.

SPECIFIC vs. VAGUE WORDS

Always use specific, concrete words when describing conditions.

For instance, instead of saying the "victim was upset," state specifically what the victim said or did that led you to form that opinion. You should say the "victim was yelling and crying while I interviewed her." The reader will form his or her own opinion based upon your descriptive, specific language.

Here are some examples:

Vague	Specific
Drunk	Falling down, bloodshot eyes, vomited on self, smelled of alcohol, slurred his words
Combative	Hit me with his fist, pushed me away
Complaint of pain	The back of his neck hurt
Injury	A cut (an opening, incision, wound, etc. made by a sharp-edged instrument) about 1 inch by 2 inches; Laceration is even more specific, meaning a jagged tear or wound, a wound having jagged edges
Nervous	Twitching, Wandering about, Sweating

HOMONYMS

A homonym is a word <u>identical</u> with another in pronunciation, but <u>differing</u> from it in spelling and meaning, as *fair* and *fare*, *read* and *reed*, *mite* and *might*, *buy* and *by*, *see* and *sea*. Most of the pairs of words on the following list are true homonyms, meaning that they are pronounced exactly alike. Those that are not have pronunciations that have changed through usage to the point where they are almost identical.

Aid / Aide	Buy / By	Dew / Do / Due
Ail / Ale	Callous / Callus	Die / Dye
Air / Heir	Canvas / Canvass	Discreet / Discrete
Aisle / Isle	Capital / Capitol	Ewe / You
Allowed / Aloud	Cash / Cache	Faint / Feint
Altar / Alter	Ceiling / Sealing	Fair / Fare
Arc / Ark	Cell / Sell	Faze / Phase
Ate / Eight	Cereal / Serial	Forgo / Forego
Bail / Bale	Choose / Chews	Fort / Forte
Bare / Bear	Chord / Cord	Forth / Fourth
Beat / Beet	Cite / Sight / Site	Forward / Foreword
Berry / Bury	Click / Clique	Foul / Fowl
Billed / Build	Coarse / Course	Grate / Great
Birth / Berth	Complement / Compliment	Guessed / Guest
Blew / Blue	Core / Corps	Hail / Hale
Boar / Bore	Council / Counsel	Hall / Haul
Board / Bored	Cue / Queue	Heal / Heel
Bolder / Boulder	Currant / Current	Hear / Here
Brake / Break	Curser / Cursor	Heard / Herd
Bread / Bred	Dear / Deer	Higher / Hire
Bridal / Bridle	Desert / Dessert	Holy / Holey / Wholly

Hour / Our	Ought / Aught	Red / Read
Idle / Idol	Overdo / Overdue	Residence / Residents
Instants / Instance	Packed / Pact	Right / Rite / Write / Wright
Its / It's	Pail / Pale	Role / Roll
Knew / New / Gnu	Pain / Pane	Root / Route / Rout
Know / No	Pair / Pare / Pear	Rote / Wrote
Knot / Not / Naught	Passed / Past	Sail / Sale
Lead / Led	Patience / Patients	Scene / Seen
Lean / Lien	Peace / Piece	Scent / Sent / Cent
Leased / Least	Peak / Peek / Pique	Seam / Seem
Lessen / Lesson	Peal / Peel	Seed / Cede
Levy / Levee	Pedal / Peddle	Sense / Cents
Lie / Lye	Peer / Pier	Serge / Surge
Loan / Lone	Plain / Plane	Shear / Sheer
Made / Maid	Pleas / Please	Shoot / Chute
Mail / Male	Pole / Poll	Shone / Shown
Main / Mane	Pore / Pour	So / Sew / Sow
Mean / Mien	Pray / Prey	Soar / Sore
Meat / Mete	Presence / Presents	Sole / Soul
Medal / Meddle	Principal / Principle	Some / Sum
Metal / Mettle	Profit / Prophet	Son / Sun
Mite / Might	Rain / Rein / Reign	Stair / Stare
Naval / Navel	Raise / Rays / Raze	Stake / Steak
Night / Knight	Rap / Wrap	Stationary / Stationery
Oar / Ore / Or	Read / Reed	Steal / Steel
One / Won	Real / Reel	Straight / Strait

Sweet / Suite	Through / Threw	Wait / Weight
Tail / Tale	Tier / Tear	Waive / Wave
Tare / Tear	To / Too / Two	Ware / Wear / Where
Taught / Taut	Undo / Undue	Way / Weigh
Team / Teem	Vain / Vane / Vein	Weak / Week
Their / There / They're	Vale / Veil	Whose / Who's
Theirs / There's	Vial / Vile	Wood / Would
Therefor / Therefore	Vice / Vise	Your / You're
Throes / Throws	Waist / Waste	

BIG WORDS vs. SMALL WORDS

Don't use a big word when a small word will do (unless you are absolutely, positively sure that the bigger word expresses exactly and precisely what you are trying to say). For example, imagine telling your son to "activate" the bedroom light. You wouldn't normally speak this way, so why write this way? You can't place complete faith in a list of synonyms. Before you use the bigger word, look it up in a dictionary. Notice that the preferred word is usually shorter, too.

NO	YES
Accumulate	Gather
Activate	Start; Turn
Additional	More
Ascertain	Learn
Cognizant Of	Know
Concur	Agree
Expeditious	Fast
Factor	Fact (The two words don't mean the same thing)
Feasible	Likely
Initial	First

71

Interface	Relate
Locate	Find
Magnitude	Size
Materialize	Occur;Happen
Necessitate	Require
Personnel	People
Prior To	Before
Substantiate	Prove
Terminate	End
Transpire	Happen

WORDY EXPRESSIONS

Don't be wordy.   Get to the point.   Again, notice how much shorter the alternative word or phrase is in comparison to the wordy expression.   In the absence of particular circumstances which require a longer phrase to convey a precise thought, the shorter word or phrase is (usually) more specific, too.

NO	YES
A great majority of ...	.. Many
A majority of ...	.. Most
A sufficient number ...	.. Enough
By the time that ...	.. When
Called attention to the fact...	.. Reminded
Due to the fact that ...	.. Because
During the month of may ...	.. In May / during May
Exactly like ...	.. Identical

Except in a small number
of cases ... . Few

For the purpose of .... To

For the reason that ... . Because

 In order to ... . To

In the course of .... During

In the event that .... If, When, Should

In view of the fact that ... . Considering

It has been brought to my

attention .... I learned

Make a determination ... . Determine

Make contact with .... Meet

Pertaining to ... . About

Subsequent to .... After, Following

With reference to / In regard to .... About

WORD CHOICE

BAD	BETTER
Informed, Notified,	Told / Said / Stated
Advised, Instructed	
Related, Explained	
Articulated, Verbalized	

Altercation, Mutual	Fight
Combat, Physical	

Verbal altercation,	Argument
Verbal dispute,	
Heated debate,	
Fiery exchange of words,	
Verbal flare-up	
Regarding, In regard to,	About
Reference, In reference to	

Due to the fact that,	Because
In view of the fact that	
In light of the fact that	

At this point	Then (Often, you need no substitute—just leave those words out)
At this time	
At which time	
At this point in time	

Utilize, Make use of,	Use
Employ	

Kept under observation	Watched
Maintained surveillance	
Over, Visually monitored	

More Poor Word Choices

The word "proceeded" is most abused in two ways:

Examples:

Bad:	I proceeded to the rear yard.
Better:	I went to the rear yard.
Best:	I ran to the rear yard.
	I walked to the rear yard.

Bad:	I proceeded to conduct an investigation.
Better:	I investigated.

Bad:	I proceeded to question the witness.
Better:	I questioned the witness.

Instead of using vague words such as "*observed*" and "*detected,*" simply <u>say what you mean</u>.

Bad:	I observed that there was a bottle on the floorboard.
Better:	I saw a bottle on the floorboard.

Bad:	I detected the odor of burning marijuana.
Better:	I smelled burning marijuana.

Another poor word is "contact." You can "contact" a witness in person, by phone, by letter, or by telegram. Each of these methods presents different problems of proof. Instead of saying that someone was "contacted," say <u>who</u> did it, and <u>how</u>.

Bad: Lewis was contacted at his home.

Better: I telephoned Lewis at his home.

Don't use the ridiculous expression *telephonically contacted* when you mean *telephoned.*

"Responded" is another overused word that can always be replaced with a shorter, more factually precise word.

Bad: I responded to First Street and Cherokee Road.

Better: I drove to the intersection of First Street and Cherokee Road.

Bad: Her mother responded to the station.

Better: Her mother drove to the station.

Bad: I responded to the security office.

Better: I walked to the security office.

REDUNDANT EXPRESSIONS

(using more words than are needed; repetitious)

Don't be redundant. Eliminate words that repeat your message.

NO	YES
Actual experience	Experience
Actual fact	Fact
Advance planning	Planning
Assembled together	Together
Few in number	Few
Final conclusion	Conclusion
First began	Began
Past experience	Experience
Personal opinion	Opinion
Point in time	Now/Then

Refer back	Refer
True facts	Facts, Truth
Blue in color	Blue

SEXIST LANGUAGE

Try to avoid gender preferences by using parallel language.

Instead of	
Men and ladies	Men and women
Man and wife	Husband and wife
Mankind	People
Manpower	Personnel
Average man	Average person
Foreman	Supervisor
Policeman	Police officer
Fireman	Firefighter
To man	To operate

BIASED LANGUAGE

Don't use words that show a bias toward races, creeds, people of certain ages, and those who are handicapped or disabled.

NOT Oriental	USE Asian
NOT Afro-American	USE African-American
NOT Colored	USE African-American
NOT Black	USE African-American
NOT Handicapped	Be specific to the disability; limped, or state that they were missing an eye; etc.

LENGTHY REPORTS

It is not unusual for reports to involve multiple officers, victims, witnesses, and suspects. Imagine a burglary that is witnessed by two officers, two citizens, and involves two suspects and a stolen vehicle. A vehicle pursuit follows when the officers try to stop the suspects fleeing in the stolen vehicle. The vehicle pursuit passes through four communities (each in a different police jurisdiction), during which five more officers become involved. Along the way, two traffic collisions occur as a direct result of the pursuit. The event finally comes to a conclusion when the suspects crash the stolen car into a police car.

As you can imagine, the completed report would be a lengthy document, requiring all of the officers to write individual reports. With all of the people involved and with all the statements required, this report could easily be over 50 pages long and might be very confusing. Consider (1) writing a brief synopsis of the report; and (2) include a legend with the report so the prosecutor (and any other reader) can track what occurred and who participated.

Writing a synopsis and using a legend makes it easy:

- For the reviewing supervisor to confirm that all reports are present and accounted for. It helps the supervisor to understand the information that the officer is responsible for in their report.

- To keep track of all paperwork when it gets processed by records and court liaison personnel.

- For the district attorney to keep track of all involved parties needed to testify.

Maps of geographical areas are useful in instances of foot and vehicle pursuits as the map allows the reader to visualize the distance traveled.

Below are samples of a synopsis and legend for the same lengthy report.

SYNOPSIS:

The burglary of the victim's vehicle was witnessed by two police officers. The two suspects were seen smashing the passenger window of the victim's vehicle. When police in their units surrounded the victim's vehicle, the suspects ran to their vehicle and drove past all of the police cars. Officers chased the suspects approximately seven miles and into two neighboring communities. During the pursuit the suspects drove on the wrong side of the street, failed to stop at red traffic signals, and collided into two vehicles being driven by citizens. The pursuit ended and the suspects were captured when the suspect vehicle sideswiped a police vehicle.

<u>LEGEND</u>

Agencies involved: Los Alamitos Police Department, Cypress Police Department, Los Angeles County Sheriff's Department, Hawaiian Gardens Police Department, and California Highway Patrol. Case number by agency:

97034877	Los Alamitos
9712347	Cypress
97-2930-887734	Los Angeles County Sheriff (serving Norwalk)
9720388	Hawaiian Gardens
CHP 9723-09-560-988998	California Highway Patrol

Original Reporting Officer: D. Smith, #567, Los Alamitos Police Department   (took original vehicle burglary report and witnessed the burglary; documented the statements of the two citizen witnesses (Iken and Smithy) and the victim (Taley);   performed crime scene investigation and collected all evidence at the burglary scene.)

Officer B. Blount, #578, Los Alamitos Police Department   (witnessed burglary of victim's vehicle and pursued the suspects in his police vehicle; witnessed Vehicle Code violations committed by the suspects; witnessed the first traffic collision caused by the suspects failing to stop for a red traffic signal; witnessed the suspect's vehicle collide with the Los Angeles County Sheriff's police car and took suspect Jones into custody; prepared map of pursuit)

Officer T. Webster, #347, Los Alamitos Police Department (involved in vehicle pursuit of the suspect vehicle; witnessed the first traffic collision caused by the suspects failing to stop at a red traffic signal; wrote the traffic collision report)

Officer S. Stanley, #290, Cypress Police Department (was involved in the pursuit once it entered Cypress' jurisdiction; witnessed various violations of Vehicle Code; witnessed the collision between the police and suspect vehicle; took suspect Neilson into custody)

Officer J. Walley, #29088, California Highway Patrol (was involved in vehicle pursuit of the suspects; witnessed various Vehicle Code violations and wrote the traffic collision report involving the suspect vehicle and the Los Alamitos Police vehicle at the end of the pursuit)

Deputy J. Quilton, #2239, Los Angeles County Sheriff's Department (was involved in pursuit of the suspect vehicle once it entered Norwalk; witnessed various Vehicle Code violations and the traffic collision between citizen Koll's vehicle and the suspect vehicle; wrote the traffic collision report involving citizen Koll and Morton and the suspects' vehicle)

Officer M. Paulsen, #211, Hawaiian Gardens Police Department (was involved in pursuit of suspect vehicle once it entered Hawaiian Gardens; witnessed various Vehicle Code violations, the traffic collision involving citizen Koll and Morton, and the collision involving the suspect vehicle and police car at the end of the pursuit)

You would continue to list each of the officers who would have a report and what their report would say. This synopsis and legend would then preface the original report written by Officer Smith, the officer who took the burglary report.

CONCLUSIONARY WRITING

For years, all of us have heard, "Don't write in conclusions; state only the facts." To a large degree, this statement is true, but it doesn't explain how unsupported conclusions in a report can get an officer into trouble. As part of their daily routine, police officers and security officers are required to make conclusions and draw inferences based upon what they have seen, heard, smelled, and touched. Any conclusion you make in a report must be completely supported by facts that are clearly, accurately, and logically stated in that report. If that isn't the case, the conclusion shouldn't be there.

You stop a car because the driver fails to stop for a posted stop sign. When you walk up to the driver, he appears nervous. If you write the report using only the previous sentence to describe the driver as nervous, your writing would be conclusionary and not supported by recorded facts, and therefore unacceptable. To rectify the situation, write down what the driver did and what you saw that led you to believe he was nervous. You might add that the person fumbled for his driver's license, his palms started to sweat, sweat beaded on his forehand, he kept looking left and right, and when you asked him a question, he jumped as though you had startled him.

You probably have heard the following, "If it looks like a duck, walks like a duck, quacks like duck, it probably is a duck" or some variation of that statement. It's most likely true, but hold that thought, and read the following two paragraphs.

Here's the scenario:

Paragraph 1:

You are driving down the street and see a man having difficulty walking. You see him stumble and almost fall at least three times. You immediately suspect that the man is either intoxicated, under the influence of drugs, or has a medical problem. Only after you stop and talk to the man, smell the alcohol on his breath and clothes, see his reddened face and bloodshot eyes, and hear his slurred speech, can you draw the reasonable conclusion that the man is probably intoxicated. Of course, the fact that the man admits to you that he drank seven 12-ounce cans of beer in the last hour provides you with conclusive information to properly infer that the man is intoxicated. If you write those facts that way in the report, you have properly supported your conclusion that the man was intoxicated.

80

However, consider this:

Paragraph 2:

It's the same setting—you're driving down the street and see a man having difficulty walking. You see him stumble and almost fall at least three times. You immediately suspect that the man is either intoxicated, under the influence of drugs, or has a medical problem. You stop and talk to him. You see his bloodshot eyes, disheveled clothing, his difficulty standing up; he smells strongly of alcohol, and his speech is slurred and mostly unintelligible. You conclude that the man is probably intoxicated, even though he mumbles "No way" when you ask him if he has been drinking (alcoholic beverages). He doesn't even admit to having had the standard "two beers." He tries to walk away, but stumbles again and almost falls into the path of passing vehicle traffic. You conclude that he's intoxicated.

Would you arrest him for being drunk in public, and put the given facts in your report to support your conclusion? You might.

But, what if (a few minutes before you see him): The man is in a restaurant having lunch with his girlfriend and discussing their relationship; he's drinking water, she's drinking a large bourbon with ice. Their discussion escalates into an argument, then a screaming match. She throws her drink in his face (with a lot of it going into his eyes), tells him she's going to cut off some of his appendages, pulls a knife out of her purse, and lunges toward him. His eyes are burning and his vision is blurry from the alcohol, which is all over his face and shirt, and he can barely see the knife and avoid the lunge she makes toward him. He's terrified, because he knows she'll do it (cut off appendages). He leaps up out of the chair, and backs away from the table and from the knife being brandished at him. He's stumbling and off-balance, moving quickly. His lunge takes him backward, over a low banister, down to the next level of the restaurant (four or five feet), where his head smacks into a table. He's unconscious for several seconds and "comes to" as his assailant is about to leap onto him, knife in hand, from the banister over which he just fell. Galvanized by terror, nearly incoherent from fear of mutilation, half-blinded by and reeking of bourbon, dazed from a mild concussion, and hearing the woman's bloodcurdling screams of rage behind him, he stumbles out of the restaurant and onto the sidewalk, where, of course, his "trick knee" gives way. The stuttering problem he had long ago overcome resurfaces as a result of the stress of the situation. That's when you see him. (Unbeknownst to him, his girlfriend decided he wasn't worth the trouble, and went home.)

Far-fetched? Of course. Possible? Certainly. Be sure of your facts, and do not jump to conclusions.

PROOFREADING AND EDITING

Learning Objectives:

- *How to edit*
- *How to proofread*
- *How to review a final checklist*

Although editing and proofreading are both concerned with details such as correct spelling and grammar, EDITING is concerned with a much BIGGER PICTURE.

When you edit, you first look at a written piece with a viewpoint of content and tone. Then you analyze the paragraphs, looking for whether they vary in length and whether you've developed the topic.   Then you examine each sentence for structure, grammar, and syntax.   Finally, you study each word, asking yourself whether it's spelled correctly and whether it's the best word for communicating your message.

When you proofread, you are concerned more with the fine details of mechanics: spelling, punctuation, overall appearance, consistency in style, and so forth.

Here are some tips for discovering all the errors in your report:

1)   Read the entire report out loud. Your eyes can be deceived by what they see, but not your ears. (When possible read out loud to someone else),   Put time and distance between what you write and what you edit.

2)   Read the entire report backwards, starting at the last line, and reading upwards to catch any spelling errors.

3)   Edit for meaning:

Simple?

Clean?

Easy to understand?

In order?

Active voice?

1st Person?

Past tense?

4) Edit for correctness:

   Are the facts correct?

   Is the spelling correct?

   Is the punctuation correct?

   Are there grammatical errors?

5) Content

   Are the elements of the crime present?

   Probable cause for stop, detention, and arrest is listed?

   Basis for search and seizure of property is established?

   Basis for entry into private residence is established?

   Penalty-enhancing circumstances are listed?

6) Paragraphs

   At least 3 per page?

   Vary in length?

   One major topic in each?

   Flow together coherently?

   Sentences flow logically?

7) Sentences

   Vary in length?

   Only one major idea in each?

8) Words

   Used simple words? Eliminated slang, jargon?

THE FINAL CHECKLIST

Proofread the report a final time to make sure that all corrections are incorporated into the submitted version. Remember, organization is the key to clarity. Make sure that the report at the very least answers the questions of who, what, where, when, why, and how.

Use plain and simple words. Avoid any word that will not be instantly understood (except when you are quoting someone word-for-word).

Keep sentences simple. Sentences that try to make two or three points usually have so many dependent and independent clauses and parentheses, etc., that you create a maze, confusing yourself and the reader.

Short sentences are usually better than long ones. One of the easiest ways to write short sentences is to give each sentence just one job. You can't make every sentence a completely accurate, self-contained statement of the facts, so don't try.

Don't be repetitive. If you said something in one paragraph, you don't need to say it again in the next paragraph, or even mention that you said it before (e.g., "As stated in the preceding paragraph...,")

Rewrite any sentence that is more than two lines long to make it shorter or to make more than one sentence out of it.

Notes:

CHAPTER 8

<u>REPORT WRITING RESPONSIBILITIES FOR SUPERVISORS</u>

In this chapter you will learn:

- *To recognize common deficiencies in written reports*
- *About ethical considerations for supervisors*

A poorly written report reflects negatively upon the person who wrote it as well as the supervisor who approved it. Supervisors should never approve a less-than satisfactory report even if it means the report needs to be rewritten three or four times.

Quality control begins with the supervisor, and most of you will eventually supervise personnel in some manner. After completing this manual, you should be able to critique any written report and offer an informed evaluation. Reviewing reports through the lens of a supervisor will not only elevate your own report writing skills, it will take your employees' writing to a whole new level and continuously improve their skills.

The responsibility of a good supervisor includes reviewing and approving reports and other documents submitted by subordinates; therefore, you must maintain your own writing skills at a high level in order to be able to recognize any deficiencies. You must be able to provide the struggling writer with recommendations and accurate corrections in order for the officer's future reports to be written correctly.

Every organization should have a report writing manual that can be provided to new officers and used as a reference. The manual should contain a copy of every report form used by the organization and an explanation of when that form is to be used and by whom. Using your organization's forms is the easiest way for new officers to become familiar with the kind of written work that is expected of them. Provide examples of written reports that are considered acceptable. (This will also eliminate confusion created by different supervisors having different report writing standards.) If your organization does not have easily recognized, tangible report writing standards, take the initiative to compile some standards on your own.

Frequently remind subordinates the importance of their written work; who will read them, how opinions are formed because of them, and how court testimony, future assignments, and even promotions may depend upon the officer's writing ability.

It is difficult to demand and expect quality if there are no clear-cut standards you can point to with confidence that reinforce your organization's expectations. Consistent, standardized writing patterns produce well written and quality reports.

Why the Problems Exist

Report writing problems may indicate: a lack of skill; laziness; carelessness; learning disability; poor supervision; and/or a lack of standards. A supervisor must recognize the important role he or she plays in an officer's success or failure in report writing, and at the same time remember that as a supervisor, he or she can only do so much. A supervisor's guidance and vigilance can help eliminate some of the causes listed in the first sentence, but there are those causes that require outside professional help (e.g., learning disability). Just make sure that as a supervisor, you're part of the solution and not part of the problem.

Mechanical Errors

Mechanical errors that most frequently appear in reports are errors in sentence structure and punctuation, use of passive voice, inappropriate use of jargon and codes, inappropriate mixed tenses, writing in the third person, poor word choice, wordiness/redundancies, and spelling errors.

Content Problems

Common deficiencies relative to content are: failure to clearly articulate probable cause for detention or arrest; failure to include all the elements of the crime; failure to document the voluntariness of admissions and confessions; failure to state the basis for search and seizure of person, vehicle, or dwelling; and failure to properly support your conclusions and inferences.

Reading Skills

Because writing skills are closely related to reading skills, it is not uncommon for an officer who writes poorly to also be a poor reader. Therefore, it makes sense that an officer needs to practice both. Encourage poor writers to read daily, whether it be a professional journal, the local newspaper, or a book. They should choose reading materials they will enjoy and that will increase their reading speed and comprehension.

Spelling

Spelling errors can be corrected by using computer software aids such as a grammar/spell-checker, and a dictionary, and thesaurus. Spelling problems, on the other hand, can be eliminated by study, practice and repetition. There is no magic cure-all. And, absent a medically diagnosed learning disability, there really are no excuses for poor spelling. Encourage your officers to keep a spelling journal of the words that regularly give them problems and to refer to it often when they are unsure of the spelling of a word or use a different word. The old "cop-out" of "How can I use a dictionary to look up the correct spelling of a word when I can't spell it in the first place?" should result in a low rating from a supervisor on that officer's evaluation in the area of report writing /communication skills.

Solutions

For most officers, <u>solutions</u> to these problems are quite simple as long as they possess basic writing skills. They need to review and brush up on their writing style. For officers who have a serious writing problem such as the inability to write a sentence that makes sense, I strongly recommend that: (1) he or she employ a tutor; or (2) take a basic or remedial English writing course at a local college (making sure that basic sentence structure is discussed and practiced in the course before you sign up). English as a Second Language (ESL) classes are offered locally at many colleges and were originally intended for immigrants, but the content of such a class is so basic, it can also be beneficial to officers with major writing difficulties.

Computers

It is becoming more common for officers to use computers when writing reports. The computer is a valuable asset and should be used whenever possible. It produces a better-looking product, and many grammar and spelling features in computer programs today can greatly aid an officer in writing a much better report. However, officers should never rely entirely on the computer to bring all of their errors to their attention. The typical computer program will not be able to determine if a word spelled correctly is properly placed in the sentence. Neither will the program be able to determine if an officer who uses a homonym (words that sound alike but have different meanings) has used the correct word. The program won't be able to help the officer put events in chronological order or prevent valuable information from being left out of the report. No computer program will correct inadequate or inaccurate notes.

Sample Reports

Sample reports are very helpful as they can help the officer choose the proper language for a particular kind of report, and can demonstrate the proper presentation of chronological order in a report. At the end of this manual is a collection of sample reports that officers can use to guide them in writing about similar incidents.

Training Officers

Since supervisors frequently have input regarding new officers and who their training officers will be, emphasis should be placed on assigning a training officer who writes well and will help his or her trainee avoid some of the major report writing pitfalls. Otherwise, expect the trainee to take on the unsatisfactory report writing skills acquired from or reinforced by the training officer.

<u>DOs and DON'Ts</u>

One of the worst mistakes that a supervisor can make in regards to a less-than-satisfactory report is to <u>point out</u> ALL the errors to the officer and then request that the officer correct the report. This teaches the officer nothing!   Instead, the supervisor should review the report and make a list of deficiencies and mistakes.   Tell the officer what types of mistakes were found (misspelled words, sentences that don't make sense, etc.) and identify the areas where the report was deficient; then have the officer find and correct the mistakes, and upgrade the deficient areas (probable cause, elements, etc.). This process, when repeated several times, will encourage most officers to edit and proofread more efficiently.

For those officers who are "borderline" writers, provide practice reports on a regular basis.

Report writing will only improve with practice!

<u>Some Final Ethical Considerations</u>

Supervisors must keep in mind certain ethical considerations of report writing. Some common traps that officers fall into are: "Inventing" probable cause to justify their actions, inaccurate chronological order of events, and misquoting statements.   Officers can easily exaggerate incidents in an attempt to justify their actions.

If a supervisor was present at the incident, that supervisor should read and approve the report.   When multiple officers are present at an incident, each officer's account should be closely examined for contradictions and discrepancies.

CHAPTER 9

INVESTIGATIVE CHECKLISTS

The following section will aid even the veteran officer in the most common types of investigations. Keep the list handy and follow it as you progress in your investigation. These are investigation tips that officers tend to forget and the results can be catastrophic to the case.

A particular checklist is not intended to cover all aspects of a criminal investigation. It primarily includes the questions that must be asked by the original reporting officer to establish that the crime occurred and to provide the reader with an accurate picture of what took place.

Always refer to your department's policy and procedure manual, and check with your local prosecuting attorney's office to ensure conformity to their procedures.

GENERAL REMINDERS

1. Note whether or not the victim desires prosecution.

2. Note if the victim(s) and witness(es) would recognize the suspect if they saw him or her again.

3. As the original reporting officer, if you are prevented from performing a reasonable and expected investigative step, state in your narrative what prevented you from doing so.

4. List ALL officers present at any investigation. In most cases, each officer should write a supplemental report (supplemental to the original reporting officer's report), stating why they were there, what they did, what they saw, etc.

5. Separate all witnesses, victims, and suspects as soon as practicable after you arrive. DO NOT interview them together and do not allow them to overhear your interviews with others.

6. For serious offenses, consider the use of an audio/video tape recording of the suspect's statement. However, do not allow the tape to take the place of good notes. The use of videotaped admissions and confessions of suspects to prove the voluntariness of statements is always beneficial.

7. In cases where businesses use surveillance equipment (video and closed-circuit television) to monitor the store's business operations, ask for the tape that would or should have recorded the view of the area during the time of the offense. Even if there is nothing on the tape useful to your investigation, a good defense attorney will attempt to show that you failed in your responsibility by not taking the tape as evidence.

8. Always include the name and address, etc., of the people that you talked to even if they don't provide you with useful information. This is especially important in canvassing neighborhoods in major crimes. It will save investigators time because they won't be talking to the same people that you already interviewed, and it helps to support your contention that you talked to everyone you could reasonably locate.

9. Always provide victims of violent crimes with information about referral groups such as rape counseling and other available local resources.

Arrest by Private Person Investigation Checklist

Most often, officers go to in-store security to accept what is commonly referred to as a "private person's arrest" for theft, burglary or trespassing. The officer accepting the arrest must make sure that the report written by security establishes the elements of the criminal section, or the officer may well be accepting an unlawful arrest.

1. Review the report written by the store's security officer(s). Confirm that the report establishes the elements of the crime that the person has been arrested for. It must list the victim, witnesses, informants, (basically, anyone who can provide relevant information relating to the incident and arrest), and their statements as to what they saw, heard, etc.

2. The officer's report should contain the date and time of arrival to accept the arrest, and any interviews that the officer conducted. Include a statement that you personally spoke to the security officer(s) and confirmed their report, observations, etc., rather than simply accepting their report on face value. DO NOT ASSUME THAT STORE SECURITY PERSONNEL WROTE A SATISFACTORY REPORT OR THAT THEY MET THEIR LEGAL RESPONSIBILITIES IN MAKING THE PRIVATE PERSON'S ARREST. READ THE REPORT!

3. Nowadays, it is common for businesses to have video surveillance equipment that captured the entire crime on tape. If this is the case, the tape is evidence and must be secured as evidence. Review the tape, and in your narrative, state what you saw. Book the tape into evidence.

4. If you had to conduct further investigation, include what you did in your narrative. If you read the suspect his MIRANDA[3] rights, state so in your report. Document the suspect's reply in your report by using his exact words. If possible, use a pre-printed MIRANDA rights form that you can read from, and have the suspect sign it. If multiple suspects are involved, do not interview them together. Each one must have their rights read to them and their comments, waivers, etc., must be accurately recorded.

5. Statements from the suspects should always answer how and why they committed the crime. Try to show intent. If there are discrepancies or contradictions between the suspects' statements attempt to establish why. Where suspects attempt to use a defense or alibi, investigate the defense or alibi to either refute or confirm their statement.

---

[3] This refers to the advisement of rights against self-incrimination, right to an attorney, etc., required to be given pursuant to *Miranda v. Arizona*, 384 U.S. 436 (1966). Follow your own department's policies and procedures regarding the advisement of Miranda rights.

6. Search the suspect and everything in his possession such as packages, boxes, etc., even if security has already done so. It's not unusual to find a theft suspect in possession of property from other victim businesses. State that you searched the suspect and document what the suspect had in his possession such as cash, credit cards, and/or checks to pay for the item he is accused of stealing. The inability to pay for the stolen items, may show intent. If you were not able to search the suspect, say so. A prosecutor will want to know if you searched the suspect and if you found anything on him, which could help to prove intent. A search is especially important if you intend to write the suspect a citation at the scene and release him without a formal booking.

7. List in your report what happened to the evidence. In many jurisdictions it is perfectly acceptable to photograph the stolen article and to return it to store security. On the property page of your report, make sure you state that the item was recovered and returned.

8. Document that you performed a warrant and criminal records check and what your findings were. In some cases, prior petty thefts can be upgraded to burglaries at the time of booking and upon filing of the case with the district attorney.

9. Always confirm the suspect's identity, especially when they have no identification on them, which is common. Photographs and fingerprints can be valuable in these cases, so care should be taken not to release the individual without photos and fingerprints when positive identification is not possible.

10. List the disposition of the suspect, if they were booked at your jail or released on a citation after booking or released at the scene.

Driving Under The Influence Arrest Investigation Checklist
Accidents:

1. Where the accident involves other vehicles and drivers, obtain their statements regarding the suspect's driving and physical behavior.

2. In ALL accidents, state how the driver is identified as the driver. In addition to the suspect's statement, there must be independent evidence to place the driver behind the wheel. *EXAMPLES*: The suspect is identified by other drivers as the suspect seen driving the vehicle upon impact. In solo accidents the vehicle may be registered to the suspect, the vehicle keys may be in the suspect's pockets, the suspect is still seated behind the wheel, blood in the vehicle is consistent with injuries on the suspect driver. ALWAYS LOOK FOR WITNESSES!

DUI Behavior Witnessed by the Officer:

1. State what driving behavior caused the suspect to come to your attention. State what vehicle code violation occurred as well as other behavior.

2. On traffic stops, state how long it took to get the driver to stop. Hit the curb? Park in the street?

3. Once stopped, state what you saw the driver do: Fumble for his driver's license, slurred speech, odor of intoxicants, etc., stumbling and so on.

4. Field Sobriety Tests: document specific behavior, skills or lack of as well as specific comments such as "I can't do that," "I'm too drunk," "Screw you—I'm doing nothin."

5. Other statements that are helpful are ones that relate to how long he was drinking before stopped, when he started drinking, how much, and type of alcohol. If there are other occupants in the car, obtain their statements, too, relative to where, how long, etc., the suspect was drinking.

6. Advise the suspect that he is under arrest and explain the requirement to submit to a blood, breath, or urine test, and note his exact words. Search the vehicle for signs of intoxication or drug use. If you don't find any say so in your report. At least your supervisor and the DA will know that you looked.

7. If you suspect that the suspect is under the influence of both alcohol and other drugs, obtain the services of a qualified narcotics officer for exam.

8. Upon consent of the blood alcohol test state who witnessed the test and results, if known, as well as the disposition of the sample.

9. State what the disposition was of the suspect.

Domestic Violence Investigation Checklist

1. Note the time of dispatch and arrival time as well as who reported it and what prompted them to call the police.

2. Note your observations upon arrival such as victim's general demeanor, condition, obvious injuries. Who was at the scene when you arrived? Describe the scene, such as furniture turned over, bloodied weapon, shell casings, etc.

3. Request medical aid and note who responded   (paramedics, their names and identification numbers). If injured party (ies) refuse medical aid record their refusal (will seek own doctor, etc.) If transported to hospital, note name and address and attending physician.   Note all injuries that you saw and any other complaint of pain.

4. Photograph all injuries to both victim and suspect. Take photos (full body shots, front and back, in original clothing, to show rips, tears, etc., as well as injuries.)   Involved parties should be re-photographed after several days, especially when bruises and other injuries are not readily apparent at time of report.

5. Victim and Witness statements: establish the relationship and the length of time they were together.   Document history and what might have led to the assault.   Is it *gang* related?   Is it a gang area?   Are the parties related? (family, etc.)   When did the relationship end?   In cases of *domestic violence*, is there a restraining order in effect? If so, did the suspect know that there was a restraining order in effect? Was the suspect served with the restraining order? Is it current

or expired? What type is it (emergency, permanent)? Note the court that issued the order and/or note the docket number. Obtain statements regarding how and why the incident occurred. (If you have a copy of the restraining order and the suspect has not been served, serve him or her.)

6. Check with your records division to see if your organization has documented previous responses to the same address or same victim and suspect for similar occurrences. If so, mention those dates, times, and case numbers in your report.

7. In cases of domestic violence note if minor children are present and obtain their statements and note their behavior (frightened, crying, etc.) Consider additional charges if you have evidence indicating that the domestic violence in the home is ongoing or if children are injured. Consider removing the children for their own protection especially in cases where you have information that the situation is ongoing. Neighbors can often provide additional information on the couple's arguments, fights, etc.

8. Collect necessary evidence such as weapons, torn clothing, and blood spatter samples.

9. Detention and arrest of suspect: If detention is involved, note the probable cause for the initial detention. If in a residence, keep RAMEY[4] in mind and note all circumstances prior to entry. If the assault involved domestic violence, RAMEY probably won't apply.

10. Infield show-ups: Note precautions taken (not overly suggestive, not too many officers present, not handcuffed, not sitting in a caged police car, etc.) Include a SIMMONS[5] advisement to all victims and witnesses making identifications, and include their statements that they understand, and that they did or did not recognize the suspect(s). List all officers present who can act as witnesses.

11. Note the circumstances under which you advised the suspect of MIRANDA rights (when, where, who else was present as well as the statements of waiver, etc.) If the suspect refuses to talk, note exactly what was said (asked for a lawyer or just didn't want to talk). State whether or not the suspect was under the influence of drugs or alcohol at the time of assault, and note behavior.

---

[4] This refers to the California Supreme Court decision in *People v. Ramey* (1976), 16 Cal.3d 263, that arrests without a warrant within the home are per se unreasonable in the absence of "exigent circumstances." Know what "exigent circumstances" means and what the "exigent circumstances" standards are for your department and your prosecutor's office.

[5] This refers to the admonishment required to be given to persons viewing a photo line-up, in order to preserve objectivity, avoid any suggestion of being pressured or influenced to identify a suspect, etc., and to make sure that the "photographic identification procedure was *not* so impermissibly suggestive as to give rise to a very substantial likelihood of irreparable misidentification." *Simmons, et al. v. United States,* 390 U.S. 377 (1968). Your prosecutor's office and/or your department should have pre-printed forms for this purpose.

NOTE (1): In most instances, officers make a major error by not attempting to get a statement from a suspect immediately after the incident. That is the time the suspect is most likely to talk and tell his side of the story. INTENT IS IMPORTANT! The longer he has to think about being in custody, the more likely he won't ever make incriminating statements. Spontaneous statements are perfectly good, as long as the reporting officer documents under what circumstances they were made and obtained.

Some organizations want their officers to wait for a detective to conduct the interview. Check with your agency first and follow its recommended procedures.

NOTE (2): The idea here is to always try to obtain a statement, confession, admission, or denial/alibi. It will be extremely difficult for the suspect to credibly change his story later. Changes in statements that do occur can often be used to impeach the suspect's credibility.

Malicious Mischief Investigation Checklist

1. Must show that the crime was done with malice. Children playing baseball and accidentally breaking a car window is not malicious mischief.

2. Be specific on the value and use the appropriate dollar section under vandalism. There are four separate sub-sections depending upon the dollar amount.

3. Spray painting: Consider taking photos in all cases of graffiti.

4. "Tagger" graffiti requires enough description if multiple incidents are to be tied together by the same tagger. Gang graffiti requires specific gang symbol(s) and any names listed.

5. Always look for the instrument which caused the damage (paint can, marker, etc.) that fingerprints could be obtained from.

Robbery and Grand Theft Investigation Checklist

1. Note time and date dispatched and arrival time at the scene.

2. Describe your observations and the environment upon arrival (two-story residence, single commercial complex, damage noted, blood, etc.)

3. Locate and isolate victims and witnesses. DO NOT ALLOW THEM TO TALK TO EACH OTHER AND DO NOT INTERVIEW TOGETHER. Statements should include how the crime occurred, suspect's exact words, actions, and demeanor. Note force and or fear used. Describe the victim's fears and emotions. Describe any injuries sustained or damage.

4. Check for the use of video surveillance cameras in business locations such as liquor stores, banks, drive-through tellers, etc. Review the tape and state your observations in your narrative. Book the tape as evidence.

5.   Proceed with collecting all evidence, fingerprints, photos, etc.

6.   For crime scenes covering a large area, consider the use of videotaping in addition to photos.

7.   Check the neighborhood for additional witnesses, strangers loitering, and unknown vehicles.

8.   In-field show-ups: Describe how conducted (not overly suggestive, not too many officers present, not handcuffed, standing outside the police car, etc.) Note SIMMONS advisement and that victims and witnesses understood the advisement by their statements. Describe their response to the show-up noting what their exact statements were.

9.   Identification, detention, and arrest of suspect: If a detention is involved, carefully note all the probable cause for the initial detention. If the suspect is in a residence, use caution with RAMEY, being sure you have exigent circumstances prior to entry.

10. Read the suspect his MIRANDA rights and note his exact waiver or refusal. Note under what circumstances the rights were given, who was present, etc. Try to get some type of statement. Quote the suspect's confession and admissions verbatim, especially noting how and why he committed the crime.

11. Note, at the time of interview, whether or not the suspect was under the influence of alcohol or drugs. Note his behavior. Be specific.

THEFT AND BURGLARY Investigation Checklist

1.   Note the time of dispatch, arrival time, who reported the incident and how the incident was reported to police.

2.   Note possible entry points, describing the door, window, etc., locks and how the premises were entered (door kicked in, lock jimmied, window broken).

3.   Once inside, what did the suspect do? Did they ransack the entire residence or go only to a specific place? Note what items were taken and from where. If known, how did the suspect exit? Is there any way for you to estimate the number of suspects or how the property was taken away? For example, vehicle tire tracks might indicate that a vehicle was used or the same type of shoe and size print might indicate that only one person was involved.

4.   Check for physical evidence such as blood from broken glass, footprints, tire tracks, fingerprints on windows and tables, etc.

5.   Proceed with collecting necessary evidence and photography.

6.   Be specific in listing stolen property. Don't forget to list damaged property as a property loss. For example, if a window is broken in an attempt to gain entry, the cost of the window should be listed in the property loss.

7.   Ask for receipts and serial numbers along with a general description of property.

8. Do a neighborhood check for witnesses. List all addresses and names of people you talked to even if they were unable to provide any useful information. This will prevent investigators from talking to the same people again, at a later date. If you are unable to do a neighborhood check for witnesses, state what prevented you from doing so. Note addresses of homes, businesses that still need to be contacted for possible information.

9. When suspects are identified or implicated, list name, nickname(s), aliases, both home and work addresses, phone numbers, friends and acquaintances, hangouts, habits (drugs, weapons), known vehicles, etc.

10. In-field show-ups: Describe how show-up was conducted (not overly suggestive, not too many officers present, suspect not handcuffed, standing next to the police car, etc.) Note SIMMONS advisement and that victims and witnesses understood the advisement by their statements. Describe their response to the show-up.

11. Identification, detention, and arrest of suspect: if a detention is involved, carefully note all the probable cause for the initial detention. If the suspect is in a residence, use caution with RAMEY.

12. Read MIRANDA rights to the suspect and note his exact response, along with who was present. Did he ask for a lawyer or just didn't want to talk? Try to get some sort of statement.

13. Describe suspect's sobriety or drug use at time of interview. If he waives his right to an attorney and provides incriminating statements, you will need to show that he willingly and voluntarily gave up his rights.

WARRANT ARREST Checklist

1. When completing the arrest/booking forms, it is important that officers list all the CURRENT data on the suspect. Oftentimes, the information on the warrant is lacking or incorrect. DO NOT automatically assume the biographical information on the warrant is correct. Verify ALL information.

2. State how you happened to come into contact with the suspect (traffic stop, detective provided the warrant to you for service, etc.)

3. When the warrant is associated with a criminal case such as robbery or burglary, try to locate the original case number and the investigator involved. Notify the investigator just in case she or he needs to interview the suspect.

STOLEN VEHICLE REPORT Checklist

No Recovery / No Arrest

1. Narrow down the time of the theft as much as possible. Who else had keys to the vehicle and could have taken it? Is there a dispute regarding ownership? Could it have been repossessed? Is there a possible named suspect? Is it insured?

2. How was the vehicle taken? Are all keys accounted for? Is there broken glass at the scene? Did the vehicle have an alarm, anti-theft bar? Is there anything about the vehicle that would make it stand out such as body damage or bumper stickers?

3. Conduct a neighborhood check for witnesses.

4. List all property inside the vehicle that was stolen with the vehicle; for example, briefcases, wallets, and cellular phones.

Recovery / No Arrest

1. How were you notified of the recovery? Dispatched or discovered by you?

2. If reported by citizen, what caused him to call police?

3. Conduct a neighborhood check for witnesses. Named suspect?

4. Examine vehicle for evidence that the suspect left behind. Can you determine how the theft was done? Describe any damage or stripped parts.

5. Collect evidence and fingerprints.

6. Include disposition of vehicle: towed, returned to owner.

Recovery / Arrest

Same as above, plus:

1. Separate all occupants; locate any witnesses in the neighborhood.

2. Interview all occupants paying particular attention to ask questions that will show that they had knowledge the vehicle was stolen.

3. Check each occupant for sobriety (drug/alcohol).

DEATH REPORT Investigation Checklist

Apparent Natural / Accidental

1. Note your arrival time and who reported the death.   Confirm the death by checking for breathing, circulation, eye reflexes, and final notification by paramedics.   How did the body come to be found? Why was the person who found the body there? What was their relationship to the deceased? Did the person who called the police touch the body or anything significant?   Notify coroner's office.

2. Carefully enter the scene, noting lights on/off both inside and out, TV off/on, windows (open/closed/locked/unlocked). Look for signs of forced entry, missing property, or criminal activity. Note last mail delivery, paper pick up, etc. Are there any signs of a recent meal?

3. Examine body, noting whether limbs were stiff/rigid, color of the skin, injuries, recent or old. Are there any signs of foul play? Is there any indication that the body was moved after death?

4. What activity did the deceased appear to be involved with preceding death (lying on sofa, reading newspaper in bed, in bath, etc.)?

5. Was the deceased under a doctor's care? List the doctor's name, phone number, etc.

6. Are there medications present? If so, list them as well as medical problems the deceased had. Note any unlawful drugs as well as alcohol present.   Any evidence of unusual behavior or habits such as auto-erotic or ritualistic. Look for pornographic material or paraphernalia, manner of dress or nudity, symbols, pictures, and paraphernalia that might be associated with ritualistic behavior.

7. Try to determine who else lives in the residence besides the deceased.   Where were they when the deceased died?   If deceased lived alone, who was the last person to see them alive?   What was the date and time they saw the deceased?   What was the deceased's condition (mental as well as physical)?

8. Contact neighbors and relatives for more information and background.   Were there any recent visitors?   Look for personal telephone books and calendars which can provide additional names of people that can provide information such as a last appointment. Check the answering machine for messages.

9. When deputy coroner arrives, note his/her name and time of arrival.   Brief them on what information you have obtained and what you have determined from your investigation.

10. When writing your report, stay away from using language such as *rigor mortis* and *post mortem lividity*, etc. Many people do not understand such terms. Simply describe what you saw such as the limbs were stiff and rigid, the skin was blue and gray, etc.

Apparent Suicide

Handle the same as above, but in addition:

1. Request photos as soon as possible. Handle the scene as a possible homicide, being cautious of where you walk and what you touch.

2. Look for evidence that would point to a suicide (gun, drugs, note, etc.). Attempt to locate tape recordings, video tapes, etc., that the deceased may have left behind, and any possible reason for suicide (family troubles, financial, etc.).

3. If emergency personnel responded to the scene, confirm that they removed only necessary used medical supplies, and list their names.

4. Are there items that could be utilized by the victim to have killed themselves such as pills, a gun, etc.?

ADULT SEXUAL ASSAULT / RAPE Investigation Checklist

1. Note how the call was received and who called (victim, neighbor, etc.) and your arrival time. Note the physical condition and appearance of the victim (torn clothing, missing clothing, and visible injuries) as well as psychological condition (crying, hysterical, in shock). The doctor examining the victim should note in his/her separate medical report what injuries the victim suffered that are not visible. Obtain a copy of the doctor's report.

2. Get photographs of the victim fully clothed in the same clothing worn at the time of the assault. Do not allow the victim to bathe or clean up before you take those photographs. Make sure the photos are taken as soon as possible, keeping in mind that bruises often do not fully appear for hours or days after an assault. Remind the victim to return to your agency for additional photos in a few days.

3. Victim's statement should include the following: Detailed description of the suspect with and without clothing (moles, tattoos, etc.).

4. Was a vehicle involved? If so, describe it in detail.

5. Does the victim know the suspect; how did they meet; is this domestic violence related? Can she give a suspect's name or will she be able to recognize the suspect if she sees him again? Was the suspect or victim under the influence of alcohol or drugs at the time?

6. Location of occurrence: does she know the address or can she take you there?

7. The victim will need to specifically describe the type of sexual assault and how many assaults occurred. It is necessary for the victim to fully describe all sexual acts and each one in detail. For instance, if the suspect raped the victim twice and anally assaulted her twice, that must be made perfectly clear in her statement. Each assault is a separate count and can be charged as such.

8. Did she change clothes, bathe, douche, or clean up in any way? If so, where is the clothing that she was wearing at the time of the offense? Don't forget that towels, blankets, tissues, etc. are also important items of evidence.

9.   Locate and interview all witnesses. Conduct a neighborhood check. Witnesses may not have actually observed the crime, but they might be able to put the suspect, his vehicle, and/ or the victim in the area. They may have seen or heard something that corroborates the victim's statement.

10.   When you locate the suspect, does he have any injuries that coincide with the assault? After MIRANDIZING the suspect, try to get a statement. Avoid using the word "rape." Given the opportunity, he might admit to consensual sex.

CHECKS / CREDIT CARD / FORGERY CASES Investigation Checklists
Non-Sufficient Funds / Closed Account Cases

1.   Who is the victim? (who suffered the loss?) Whose name is imprinted on the check?

2.   What is the name of the bank, its location, and the victim's account number?

3.   How much is the loss? Is there a known/named suspect? Include any witnesses and their statements.

4.   To whom was the check presented? Was it accepted (date, time, place)? Did the suspect say anything upon presentation? Was ID requested, shown? What type of ID was it? Was a photo and or prints taken? Refused? Was suspect seen filling out any part of the check, including the endorsement? Did the suspect have more than 1 check? Did he have a checkbook? What did the suspect get for the check? List the goods, services, or money.

5.   If the check was passed at a commercial checking cashing company, did the suspect have a card on file with the company or have a completed application?

6.   If the check was passed at a bank or credit union, identify the teller's stamp and obtain the teller's statement. Did the teller see the suspect write any part of the check? If the check was deposited, to what account? Who is the signatory on that account?

7.   Would any of the witnesses such as the teller recognize the suspect if seen again, such as in a photo line-up?

8.   Was the bank account verified as insufficient funds or a closed account?

Forgery

Follow the suggestions noted above and clarify the following:

1.   Was the check stolen or lost? If so, how and when was it stolen or lost? How did the suspect obtain the check? Was there a stolen or lost report filed, by whom and when? What is the case number of the report?

2.   How many checks were stolen or lost? Were any other checks cashed? Who are the payees?

3.   Was the true named party on the check contacted and signature verified as a forgery? Does the true named party know the suspect? What relationship, if any? Note how you verified that the check was forged.

100

NARCOTICS / UNDER THE INFLUENCE CASES

1. How were you notified or made aware of the crime? Dispatch sent you to a call, you happened to see the suspect behaving unusual, etc.? If a citizen called and reported the suspect, obtain their statement as to what caused them to call the police.

2. Describe your first observations, prior to contact. What did you see, hear, etc., that caused you to believe the person was under the influence of some substance? (smoking a crack pipe, etc.) Note any types of violations (criminal, vehicular, or pedestrian) that the suspect committed and that you witnessed.

3. Note physical symptoms that you observed while talking with the person, such as slurred speech, poor balance, time and space distortion, odor, etc. Did you conduct any field tests? If so, describe what they were and the subject's reaction to each. Did you have a follow-up officer witness the tests? If so, list that officer as a witness.

4. Once arrest has been made, MIRANDIZE the subject and obtain a statement regarding his drug use. What drug(s) did he use? How was it used (ingested, injected, etc.)? How much (cost and weight) does the suspect use a day? How does the subject get the money to pay for his drug habit? Where and how does he obtain his drugs?

Possession of a Controlled Substance

If applicable, ask the same questions as noted above, plus:

1. How were the drugs found? (seen in plain view, pat-down search, consent search, etc.)

2. Were the drugs Valtox tested (in-the-field chemical test used by many law enforcement agencies to identify on-site commonly seized drugs such as cocaine, hashish, amphetamines, marijuana, methamphetamines, etc.)? If so, what were the results? Note the weight of the drugs.

3. MIRANDIZE the suspect and obtain a statement from him or her.

Possession for Sale

Same as above, plus the following:

1. Note if the location of arrest is a high frequency narcotic area. State how you know this information (personal experience based upon other drugs arrests that you've made and information from your department's narcotic personnel, etc.)

2. Include what you saw of the suspect's activity such as frequent short visits with vehicles or pedestrians, any gestures or physical actions which could be transactions, and count the frequency of these within a certain amount of time, if possible.

3. Check the suspect for signs of drug use such as injection marks, white powdery residue in nose, etc. Does he admit to use himself? Is he in possession of any ingestion paraphernalia?

4. Did you locate any packaging materials? Does the suspect possess cash or records of customers? Note the total amount of cash, the number and amount of each denomination of bills.

5. Were there other people with the suspect? Are they also suspects or were they there to buy or try to buy drugs? Obtain their statements as to how they know the suspect, where they met, how much do they buy, etc.

6. MIRANDIZE and obtain a statement.

Sales or Transportation of a Controlled Substance

Same as above, plus:

1. Describe the hand-to-hand sale to an officer or informant who will testify. Document the entire transaction conversation between the purchaser and suspect.

2. Document officer's observations corroborating informant or other officer.

3. If marked money is recovered, document from where and/or who.

4. For transportation case, state where the drugs/cash was found in the vehicle (hidden or in plain view)?

5. MIRANDIZE and obtain statement.

Notes:

As a criminal justice professional, you will encounter a variety of scenarios, some of which can be chaotic and emotional; however, it is vital to capture and document all of the facts presented to you at the scene. A police report is important in helping to refresh the memory of an officer who will testify in court months or even years after the incident.

Immediately following an incident, thorough and accurate details establish credibility of the first responder and provide a permanent record of information which will eventually be used and reviewed by prosecutors and the defense for court. Elements contained within the report should be the Five W's (Who What Where When Why) which are essential in providing a factual account of what occurred.

The following pages contain scenarios and information you will use to develop your report. The established guidelines below will assist in improving your writing skills and ensure a well-written report.

Guidelines for Writing Practice Reports:

1. Utilize an active voice when writing the practice reports, employing past tense when necessary.

2. Use proper language; do not use slang, jargon or police codes unless you explain what it means.

3. Read the entire scenario before you begin to write. Remember to paraphrase unless it is absolutely necessary to quote the person verbatim.

4. Facts may be out of order. It is your responsibility to put the facts in the correct order.

5. Determine what information is necessary and related to the crime; eliminate any unnecessary information.

6. Write the report using only the information provided. **Do not add information. The *narrative* is to be based ONLY on the information given on the sheet marked "Practice Report."**

7. You are to write only the narrative. Assume you have already written the first page. It is not necessary to repeat information already provided on the first page (face sheet).

8. There is information missing from just about every report in the following appendix. In the notes area provided, or on a separate piece of paper, note what information you think should have been added to the scenario to make your investigation more complete. State the information or the questions that should have been asked to raise the level of the investigation.

9. After you have finished writing your report, critique your work and look for areas that require improvement.

Victim: Robert Wheaton

You are working patrol today.   At 0930 hours you are dispatched to 12349 Sycamore Street, Cypress, regarding a bike that had been stolen from the victim's driveway.   You arrive at 0936 hours.   The victim, Robert Wheaton, tells you: "I had my bike parked in my driveway this morning about 8:00 am.   I had just gotten back from an early ride and picked up my morning papers at the 7-11 store just down the street.   I didn't lock my bike because I only intended to be inside the house for a couple of minutes.   My wife and I started talking and I forgot about the bike being unlocked.   Anyway, I guess it was probably about 8:15 a.m. when I came back outside to the driveway and the bike was gone.   I didn't see anyone around so I have no idea who might have taken the bike.   It's a black Schwinn 10-speed.   I don't have the serial number handy but I can probably find it on the receipt.   I'll have to check on that and let you know later.   I would say the bike was worth about $125.00.   Oh, by the way, my USC sport jacket was on the back of the bike, too.   It's a male letterman's jacket, size 46, burgundy and gold, with USC on the back.   It's worth about $150.00."

He is willing to prosecute.

Notes:

Victim: Joseph Mante

Witness: John McMillan

Date and time crime occurred: Today at 1800 hours

Location crime occurred: 4567 Katella Ave., Cypress, parking lot of Ramada Inn

Date and crime reported to the police: Today at 1815 hours

You are dispatched to take a theft report.   You arrive at 1822 hours.   The victim says that he parked his pickup truck, a blue, 1991 Dodge Ram Truck (no shell), California license 456 FFH, in the parking lot of the Ramada Inn at 1800 hours. His gardening tools were in the truck bed. The items were locked with a motorcycle chain that was secured with a combination lock.

Items stolen were: a Sears gasoline-powered mower (unknown serial number), valued at $450; a Sears gasoline-powered edger (unknown serial number), valued at $120; a Honda mini-generator, gasoline-powered (unknown serial number), valued at $400.

The victim tells you that he was made aware of the theft by his friend, the witness, who is also the bartender at the Ramada Inn.   The witness was in the process of leaving work and saw the suspects tampering with the victim's truck and equipment.   The witness ran back inside the bar and told the victim what he saw. The victim ran outside to the parking lot in time to see a truck driving away with his property in the back of it. The truck was a Chevrolet, no shell, dark blue, with tailgate damage (dent).   He got only a partial license plate of California 123_ _ _ _.   The truck looked to be about 3 to 4 years old.   The victim could only see one suspect clearly, the passenger, who looked back at the victim as they drove away.   The passenger suspect was described as a Hispanic male about 20 to 24 years old, with dark hair, and wearing a white shirt. The victim cannot describe the passenger's build or height or weight because the suspect was seated in the truck when he saw him. He cannot provide much information on the suspect driver except to say he thought the driver was a male. The victim believes that he could recognize the one suspect and the vehicle, but not the other suspect.   The victim is willing to prosecute.   He adds that the witness had to leave the scene but would be available later this date for an interview.

Notes:

Victim: Allen Talbot

You are sent to 24909 Mayberry Road, your city, to take a residential burglary report.   You arrive at about 1748 hours. The victim tells you "I locked all the doors and windows to my house this morning when I left for work at about 7:45 a.m. I came home about 5:30 p.m. and found the front door open. When I went inside, I found that someone had torn my house apart. The furniture was overturned, drawers were emptied onto the floor, and clothes were removed from the closets. I checked my dresser in the master bedroom and found approximately $300 in cash missing. I see that the scums took my Rolex watch, too. It was on the night table by my bed."

You inspect the house and see that the sliding glass door to the master bedroom has been pried. There are indentations on the metal part of the door near the lock and a screwdriver lies nearby on the patio deck. The rest of the house is a mess. Every room has been ransacked. You check with the nearby neighbors, but no one saw anyone suspicious.   He will prosecute. You call for a crime scene investigator and Officer Smith arrives to check for fingerprints. He will write a separate report regarding his findings.

The only thing confirmed stolen besides the cash is the Rolex watch valued at $4,500.00.

Notes:

Victim: Mary Paquin
Witness: Allen Foster

You are dispatched to 1239 S. Dilly Street, your city, to take a vehicle burglary report.   You arrive at about 12:22 a.m.   The burglary occurred at 11:50 p.m. in the victim's driveway. Entry was through the driver's side window, which was smashed.

The victim tells you that she was awakened just before midnight because her dog, Maxx, was barking.   As she started to get up out of bed, she heard glass breaking and ran to the kitchen window, which looks out onto the driveway.   The dog continued to bark and she heard footsteps running away from her house, but did not see anyone.   Her neighbor, Allen, called her on the phone and told her that he was startled by the same noise of glass breaking.   He looked out his kitchen window to see a male running away from the victim's car. The victim called police. She is willing to prosecute.

The witness tells you that he was watching TV in his den when he heard glass breaking. He went to the kitchen window and saw a male exiting the driver's door of his neighbor's car and it looked like the person was holding something. He ran from his house and yelled at the person to stop, but the person ran eastbound on Dilly towards a waiting vehicle and got into that vehicle on the passenger side.   He can describe the suspect vehicle only as a compact pick-up truck with a right rear tail light out. It was a dark color pick-up truck and he could not see a license plate or who was driving. The only description he can give of the suspect that he saw was a male of unknown race, with long dark hair past the shoulders, wearing all dark clothing, about 6 feet tall and weighing about 140 pounds.   He would not recognize the suspect if he saw him again.

You check the victim's vehicle and see that the driver's side window has been smashed.   The compact disk player has been removed from the dash.   There are wires hanging down from the dash. There are pliers sitting on the floorboard. The victim says the pliers are not hers. You take the pliers as evidence and book them under tag #29277.

You call for a crime scene investigator, and technician Mitchell,   #387, responds to take fingerprints.   He will write a separate report.   The CD player is an in-dash Kenwood radio combination valued at $500. The serial number is unknown. The victim's vehicle is a 1991 Ford Tempo, 2-door, California license 1FGH987.

Notes:

Victim: Fred Jackson

On today's date at approximately 1010 hours, you are dispatched to a burglary investigation at 1527 E. 103rd St.   When you reach the location, you are met by a black male who identifies himself as Fred Jackson.   Mr. Jackson tells you that he is the owner of Fred's Gun Shop at that address.   He says "I'm tired of getting ripped off.   This is the 3rd time this year I've been robbed. I just installed new locks like you guys told me to do and those creeps still got in."   He says he locked the shop the night before at about 1830 hours.   He returned this morning at 1000 hours to open up.

Fred Jackson says "I unlocked the front door with my key and immediately noticed that the front display counter had been smashed.   That counter is ten feet long and four feet high and two feet wide.   It'll cost me at least $300 to fix the counter case.   There's glass all over.   Those thieving morons took three Colt .45 caliber semi-automatic government model handguns.   I checked all of my other stock and the only other thing missing is a Buck hunting knife.   Those handguns were blue steel, model 1911A1.   The knife has a 4" folding blade and a brown and white bone handle. They were all locked in the case.   The guns are $275.00 each and the knife is $29.50."

You inspect the premises and see that the metal rear door to the business is open 3 inches.   The deadbolt lock is still in the locked position and the door jamb is bent away from the lock itself. You see at the jamb and door edge two pry marks measuring about 1" each.   The victim says that the door will cost $75 to fix.   You take 2 latent fingerprints from the exterior portion of the door. You book the fingerprints into evidence under tag #3456.

Mr. Jackson does not have the serial numbers to the missing guns readily available.   You give him a supplemental property loss sheet and tell him to fill it out and send it to the police department.

After you leave the crime scene, you stop by the only other business, which is located just south of the victim's shop, to talk to any possible witnesses.   The address there is 1525 E. 103rd St., the store is Marv's Fishing Bait and Flies.   A note on the door says the store is closed and Marv is gone fishing and won't be back until next month.

Notes:

Victim: Paul Virt

Witness: Betty Jo Virt

Suspect: Joseph Muldoon

Injuries: Swollen left ankle; refused medical aid

You are called to the victim's residence to take a report of an assault and battery. You arrive at 1500 hours. When you get there, the victim tells you that he was watering his front lawn when the suspect approached him, accusing him of letting his dog defecate on his (the suspect's) front lawn. The victim says that the suspect yelled, "Look you____, your dog crapped all over my lawn." The victim denied that his dog defecated on his lawn and the suspect went back inside his residence and came back a few minutes later with a broom. The suspect began screaming at him, referring back to the dog defecating on his lawn, and swung at the victim with the broomstick. The victim was able to deflect the broom with his left leg and ankle area, and took the blow on his leg. The victim was struck once only. He then ran into his house and called the police. The suspect ran into his house after the attack. You look at the victim's leg and it is red and starting to swell. The victim does not desire prosecution.

Witness Virt: she is the victim's wife and saw the attack from the kitchen window, about 35 feet from the front lawn. She couldn't hear what they were arguing about but could hear the suspect yelling at her husband and then saw the suspect leave, come back with a broom, and saw the suspect hit her husband's left leg with the broom.

Both the victim and his wife know the suspect as their neighbor and provide you with his name and address.

The suspect says that he did hit the neighbor's leg, believing that the neighbor's dog was responsible for pooping on his lawn. He apologized for the incident and says that he just lost his job and was upset about finding poop on his lawn. He says that the incident will not happen again.

Notes:

Victim: Sally Bowers (wife)

Suspect: Marvin Bowers (husband)

You are working patrol today and are dispatched to a domestic dispute at 1239 Leon Street, Cypress. You arrive at 1945 hours. Your follow-up officer, Smith, #212, arrives at 1946 hours. While you talk with the victim, Officer Smith stands by with the suspect.   The victim says: "I called you.   I got home from work about ½ hour ago to find my 'jerk' husband drinking again. He was in a really rotten mood and I asked him what was wrong and he said that he was fired from work today.   I told him that I wasn't surprised because he is always drinking too much. He got really angry at me and when I turned to walk away he grabbed my arm and spun me around. Then he slapped me in the face and it knocked me to the floor. I went into the bathroom and saw that I was starting to get a black right eye. I called you because I'm tired of him beating up on me—this is not the first time, you know, but I'm afraid of him.   I don't want him arrested—that'll only make things worse."

The victim refuses your offers of medical care.   You see the beginnings of a bruise around the victim's right eye.   It is already turning black-and-blue.   You take a photograph of the eye.   You provide the victim with Domestic Violence form, #209, which provides the victim with information on shelters, counseling, and the right to make an arrest.

You read the Miranda advisement to the suspect and he   says, "she had no business calling you guys-I told her that I got fired and she started calling me names and a 'drunk'. I never hit her-she hit her face on the door when she stormed out of the room.   She's a bitch and she's always bitching about something and calling me names.   She can go to hell.   I'm going to file for divorce."

You arrest the suspect and charge him with violation of California Penal Code Section 273.5, Spousal Abuse.

Notes:

Victim: Marla Downs

Station Owner and Victim: Steve Due

Reporting Party: Thomas Moody

You are working patrol today and are dispatched to a "211 gas station that just occurred" at 3434 Denni Street. You get the call at 2345 hours and arrive at 2348 hours. When you arrive, the cashier, Downs, tells you that when the suspect in the robbery was leaving, he put tape on her mouth and tied her hands. The suspect then laid her down in the bathroom which is inside the station. She had been in that position for about 5 minutes when she heard Moody calling out "Anyone here?" She couldn't yell, but she started to kick the bathroom door and Moody came to her rescue. He untied her and took the tape off of her mouth. She then called the police.

Downs continues to tell you that she was working alone this evening at the station as the cashier. She saw a pedestrian, the suspect, approach from the east and come into the station. He walked around for a few minutes looking at the candy bars and magazines. She was on the phone with the station owner about the same time the suspect walked in. When she got off the phone, the suspect turned around and faced her, pointing a gun at her. He said, "Give me all the money and fast." She opened the register and started to hand him the bills but he said, "Put it in a brown paper bag." She placed the cash in a small brown paper bag. She thinks he got about $100 (all different bills) or less because she had just made a night drop of the day's earlier receipts.

He told her to go into the bathroom (there's only one inside the station). She did so, and he followed her. When she reached the bathroom door, he told her to turn around and to put her hands behind her. She did so, and he tied her wrists with a thick type of twine. When he finished tying her wrists, he put tape over her mouth. She adds that he must have brought the tape and twine with him, because the station has no such items. He then told her to kneel down and when she did, he laid her on her side. He then closed the bathroom door. Within a second or so she heard the glass front door close and a few minutes after that she heard Moody calling to her. She is not injured and doesn't think she would recognize the suspect if she saw him again. She did not hear any cars drive away. Her best estimate of when the crime occurred was 2335 hours. She added that the suspect seemed very calm.

She can't be very specific about the gun the suspect had because she is not very familiar with handguns. She noticed it was chrome, but can't tell you if it was an automatic or revolver or how big it was. She thinks that the suspect may have touched the outside of the bathroom door around the doorknob and also the cashier's counter top. The suspect did not have any gloves on. She added that she discovered, just prior to your arrival, that the suspect apparently stole her purse, too. She had left it behind the counter on the floor and it is now gone. She describes the purse as a brown leather shoulder bag with strap, value $15.00; contents of the purse were the wallet, with only loose cash, about $20 in miscellaneous bills; brush and comb, value $5; unopened pack of cigarettes, value $3; gold cigarette lighter, value $25.

Moody says he pulled into the gas station to get gas and went into the station to give the cashier his credit card. He waited around for a couple of minutes and no one appeared. He yelled out "Anyone here?" and that's when he heard the victim kicking the bathroom door. He opened the bathroom door, saw that she had been tied up, and freed her. She then called the police. He did not see anyone else in or about the area of the gas station at anytime.

Your observations: you do a walk-through with the victim and she shows you where the twine and tape are still on the bathroom floor where she left them. You collect both and book them under the following tag numbers: twine, #12390; tape, #12391. You go outside and check the parking lot area for any evidence, and find the cashier's purse in a trash can that's behind the gas station. The only item missing from the purse is the cash. You return all the items to Downs. You call for a crime scene investigator and Officer Robin arrives and handles collecting the fingerprints. He will have a supplemental report.

Both victims (the store owner and the clerk) are willing to prosecute. She gives you the description of the suspect: male Caucasian, 20-23 years old, 5'-9", 165 pounds, black hair combed straight back (collar length), unknown color eyes, wearing a white t-shirt, black slacks, unknown shoes, and dark sunglasses.

Notes:

Victim: Lucky Supermarket

Victim: Mary Byers

Witness: Molly Smith

You are working patrol today and are dispatched to Lucky Supermarket at 11390 Salton Sea Drive for a robbery report. You arrive at 0735 hours. You are met by the store manager who is also the victim, Mary Lynn Byers. She tells you the following:

"I got here around 7:30 this morning because we open at 8 and I have to figure the cash drawers before everyone else, the clerks and so forth, get here. The clerks and stock boys get here at 7:30. Well, anyway, I came in the front door like I always do. I locked the doors behind me and I turned off the alarm and nothing looked out of place as far as I could tell. Well, anyway, I walked to the back of the store where the office is, and where the safe is. I heard a noise behind me and I turned around to find a guy with a great big knife pointing it at me and telling me to hurry and open up the safe. In fact I recall exactly what he said. It was 'Hurry up, bitch, and open the safe.' I saw that he was really nervous because he was sweating and shaking the knife like crazy. I opened up the safe and I heard some knocking on the front doors, which I knew had to be a clerk or a stock boy because it was close to 7:30. I handed the cash to him. Anyway, he heard the knock, too, and got really mad and scared and yelled at me asking for the nearest exit. Well, the front doors were still locked, and the back door, which is in the office, was still locked and had a bar over it that was also locked. You can look—the bar is still in place."

"I started to unlock the back door for him, but he grabbed me and started pulling me towards the front doors, all the time holding the knife real close to my throat. He kept saying over and over 'Don't give me a reason to cut your throat, lady. I will, I got nothin to lose.', and that's when I saw Molly standing at the door. She saw him and she started to scream. He yelled at her to shut up and for me to unlock the front doors. I did, and he went running out the doors, southbound on Salton Sea. I didn't see where he went from there. No, I'm not hurt, just scared."

She is confident that she would be able to recognize the suspect and is desirous of prosecution.

The victim also tells you that she has no idea how the suspect entered the store, as he was apparently there when she arrived. She can only give a rough estimate of how much money he got because she'll have to look at the last night's receipts before she can estimate what exactly is missing. She thinks that the amount is approximately $2500 cash (all different bills: 1s, 5s, 10s, and 20s). She tells you the suspect was a male Hispanic, about 20-25 years old, black hair slicked back, about 6' tall, weighing about 145 pounds, wearing a white t-shirt, black Levis jacket, black Levis jeans, and white tennis shoes. The suspect had a very slight limp. The suspect placed the money in the left front pocket of the jacket he was wearing.

Byers takes you on a tour of the store so you can determine how the suspect made entry. You walk into the warehouse located at the rear of the store and find that a roof vent cover has been removed. There are several boxes stacked one on top of each other allowing someone to climb up to or down from the roof vent. The victim says that the vent cover is never off and that it wasn't like that when she closed the store the night before at 11:00 p.m. She says she would have noticed the stacked boxes and the open vent on the walk-through of the building she does every night before she closes, just to make sure that all employees and patrons are out of the store. She adds that she doesn't think the vent is hooked up to the alarm system.

You advise other nearby police cars of the suspect's description. However, they are unable to locate any possible suspects. You call for a crime scene investigator to check for fingerprints on certain surfaces within the store that the suspect may have touched. Officer Brown will handle all the crime scene investigation and collection of evidence, and he will have a separate report.

Next, you talk to witness Molly Smith. She tells you, "Well, I tell you the whole sight just scared the poop out of me. I saw this guy holding a knife, a real big knife, at Mary's throat. I didn't know he was inside with her already, because I only saw her car in the parking lot, so I knew she and I were the only ones here. Anyway, I started knocking on the front doors like I always do, and next thing I know she comes to the doors with this guy. I must've started screaming because he started yelling and I saw Mary trying to open the doors with her keys. Once the doors were opened, he pushed past me and I got a real good look at his face. I would know him anywhere."

Witness Smith provides you with this suspect description: male Hispanic, about 25 years old, black hair, 5'-7" to 5'-9" tall, 150-160 pounds, wearing a white T-shirt and black pants.

Description of the store: the store is located in a commercial complex and is a single story building. There are neighboring businesses on each side of the building and an alley that runs behind the store. The alley borders the railroad tracks. The store has one set of double front doors which are locked with a dead bolt lock that requires a key to lock and unlock from the inside or the outside. The rear door has a solid metal horizontal bar which is still in place and is still locked with a combination lock. All doors and windows are hooked up to the alarm which is a burglary alarm only. The alarm is monitored through WestPac Alarms.

Notes:

#10. PRACTICE REPORT — ROBBERY, ASSAULT WITH A DEADLY WEAPON, ATTEMPT AUTO THEFT, BURGLARY

Victim: Thomas Smythe

Witness #1:   Jonathan Stanley

Witness #2:   Marvin Jaclin

You are dispatched to an assault with a deadly weapon (ADW) investigation at Albertson's food market, 1246 S. Crescent Drive, Huntington Beach.   When you get there, you are met by the two witnesses. The victim, Smythe, has a bleeding wound in his upper left thigh and he is lying on the ground.   The paramedics are already there and are attending to the victim's injuries.   The victim's injuries are not life threatening and the paramedics allow you to question the victim about the circumstances of his injury. You can see the wound and it appears to be a bullet wound.

The victim tells you that he and his roommate, Witness #1, Stanley, were at the market doing their weekly grocery shopping.   Once inside the store, the victim realized he had left his wallet in the glove compartment of his car.   The victim returned to his car leaving the witness inside the store, shopping. When the victim got to his car, he saw an unknown male Mexican adult inside the car. It appeared that the person was trying to start the car. The victim walked up to his car and yelled at the suspect to get out of his car. The suspect bolted out of the driver's door and the victim tried to grab onto him to stop him.   The two of them fell to the ground, punching each other.   Suddenly and without any warning, the suspect pulled a gun out from the jacket he was wearing, pointed it at the victim, and fired the gun, hitting the victim in the thigh. The suspect fled on foot westbound through the parking lot and onto westbound Ward Street. The victim said that this occurred about 10 minutes prior to your arrival.

You immediately announce a broadcast of the suspect's description for nearby police units.   The victim describes the suspect as a male Hispanic, about 22-25 years old, 5'-9" tall, 165-175 pounds, unknown color eyes, black hair, wearing a white T-shirt, brown leather aviator jacket, blue jeans, and unknown shoes.   The victim can describe the gun as a chrome revolver, possibly a 4 inch revolver. The victim would recognize the suspect if he saw him again and will prosecute.

Witness Stanley said that he was wondering what was taking the victim so long just to get his wallet. As the witness walked outside, he heard the shot and saw his roommate fall to the ground. He did not see the victim and suspect struggling on the ground.   He ran to the victim and saw the suspect run westbound from the area and westbound on Ward St.   He could only describe the gun as a chrome revolver. The witness said that he believed the suspect description given by the victim was correct but he added that he thought the suspect had been wearing a baseball hat that was green with white unknown lettering on the front of the hat. He says he would be able to recognize the suspect if he saw him again.

Witness #2, Jaclin, said he was in the parking lot loading up his truck when he saw the suspect and the victim struggling on the ground. The witness started to run to the victim's aid and heard the shot. He saw the suspect run westbound on Ward Street. The witness agrees with the description of the suspect that was provided, except he can't recall the clothing the suspect was wearing. He confirms the suspect was male, Hispanic, about 20-25 years old, between 5'7" and 5'10" tall, weight between 150-175 pounds, black hair, and unknown eye color.

Paramedic Winchell, #346, tells you that the victim's injury is a through-and-through gunshot wound of the thigh which will require additional medical attention. Medix ambulance will transport the victim to Huntington Beach Memorial Hospital at 12398 Lakeshore Drive, Huntington Beach.

Before you leave the scene you inspect the victim's vehicle. You see it is parked on the east side of the market. It is a 1993 Cadillac El Dorado ITS, License CBASIC, all black, and is registered to the victim. You see that the driver's window is broken out and the ignition has been pulled from the steering column. There is a screwdriver on the floor of the car near the accelerator pedal. You can't find the victim's wallet in the glove compartment. The glove compartment door is open.

Before the victim is taken to the hospital, you ask him about the screwdriver. He says that the screwdriver is not his. He also tells you the car was locked up, the windows were rolled up and the vehicle was in perfect order when he parked it. You request a crime scene investigator to take photos of the vehicle and to collect all evidence.

Notes:

Victim: Marion David

Reporting Party: Ken Mathis

You are working patrol today and are dispatched to 10933 South Street regarding an attempted suicide. Dispatch tells you that the person who attempted suicide is Marion David, who supposedly lives at the address.   The reporting party is a hot-line volunteer, Ken Mathis, of United Churches Suicide Hot Line, located at 278 N. Wilshire, Anaheim. Mathis tells your dispatcher that David had called the hot line and had told the volunteer that she was planning on killing herself with sleeping pills. Mathis kept David on the phone long enough to trace the call through the telephone company and discovered that David was calling from an address in your city.

You arrive at 0930 hours and the follow-up officer, Officer S. Parker, #3645, arrives at 0931 hours. You knock on the front door of the residence and David comes to the door and lets you in. She tells you she is extremely depressed and has been talking to a hot-line. The phone is still off the hook and Mathis is still on the line. While Officer Parker sits with David, you talk to Mathis, who confirms all the information already provided to you.

David tells you that she is depressed because of her father dying in a boating accident two days ago in San Francisco.   Her father was her only living relative and now she claims to have no one else locally who cares about her. She says her old boyfriend, Sam Horner, and she broke up about two months ago when she caught him fooling around with an old girlfriend. David says that for the last two years she has been seeing a psychiatrist for depression and has been taking two medications. Her doctor is Dr. Jerry Bump, phone # 310-388-9990.   She admits to taking all the pills in the two medication bottles. You check the containers left on the counter in the kitchen and both are empty. One bottle is marked Valium and the other is marked Paxil.

You request paramedics, who arrive and treat the victim at the scene for ingestion of the pills. The victim has now become incoherent, possibly due to the medication. She is mumbling and cannot tell you anything else.   The paramedics transport David to the hospital, Charter Hospital, 2233 N. Lemon St., for further treatment. The attending physician is Dr. Jake Halls. He pumps her stomach and tells you that due to the circumstances of the attempt suicide he will admit her to the hospital for mental evaluation by the hospital's psychiatric staff.   You complete the Welfare and Institutions Code Section 5150[4] form which states that the victim is a danger to herself.   You leave her in the custody of the doctor.

4 California Welfare and Institutions Code Section 5150 states, in pertinent part: "5150. When any person, as a result of mental disorder, is a danger to others, or to himself or herself, or gravely disabled, a peace officer, member of the attending staff, as defined by regulation, of an evaluation facility designated by the county, designated members of a mobile crisis team provided by Section 5651.7, or other professional person designated by the county may, upon probable cause, take, or cause to be taken, the person into custody and place him or her in a facility designated by the county and approved by the State Department of Mental Health as a facility for 72-hour treatment and evaluation."

Victim: Daryl Bothom

Witness: David Ramsey

Today at 0735 hours while working patrol, you are dispatched to a possible suicide at 12234 Matson Drive, La Palma. You arrive at 0740 hours and meet the witness, Ramsey, who is waiting for you as you drive up. He tells you that the victim is inside the house. Officer Smith, #234, arrives as your backup officer and the two of you quickly check the residence for any other people; there are none and you secure the residence. You quickly check for signs of life in the victim and find none. The paramedics arrive at about the same time you do.

Ramsey says he has known the victim for about 5 years. They are next-door neighbors. Ramsey had gone to the victim's residence at 7:30 a.m. The two had made arrangements to go golfing today and they were supposed to meet at 7:15 a.m. · Ramsey telephoned the victim at about 7:15 a.m., and when he didn't answer, he went next door. When he knocked on the victim's front door there was no answer. He tried the door knob and the door was unlocked. He walked into the living room and found the victim on the floor. He looked dead. He saw that the victim had a bloody head and saw the gun near the victim. He used the phone in the kitchen to call the police. He touched nothing else in the residence or on the body.

Ramsey says he talked to Bothom the night before at about 1800 hours. They confirmed their golf date. Ramsey says that he lives next door and heard nothing unusual all night and saw no one at the residence other than the victim. Ramsey has no knowledge of anyone else living at the residence with the victim. He knows of no reason why the victim would kill himself, other than the fact that he had been out of work for about 8 months. Ramsey does not know of any relatives, girlfriend, etc.

Station 21, Orange County Fire Authority, Engine #16, Paramedics John Dixon, #23, and Mark De Gaulle, #298, respond. They pronounce the victim dead at 0744 hours. At 0744 hours you call for a deputy coroner.

You see what appears to be the beginning of rigor mortis on the body. Blood has coagulated on the victim's left temple and on the floor. You see what appear to be deposits of black powder on the temple, surrounding the entry wound. The victim is lying on his back with his head facing northeast. There is a handgun in the victim's left hand and his index finger is still surrounding the trigger. There are splatters of blood on the handgun. The victim is fully clothed in a pair of blue Levi's, tennis shoes and socks and a white T-shirt. The T-shirt has blood on it. You don't see any injuries on the body except for the head wound.

On a nearby coffee table you see a box of .38 caliber ammunition. The box is open. You also see a leather handgun carrying case on the table. The residence is a single story house, with three bedrooms, a kitchen, and two bathrooms; there is an unattached garage. You check the house and all the doors and windows appear to be intact. A rear door and all windows are still locked. The residence is tidy and appears to be clean. Nothing is out of order. You do not find a suicide note.

A vehicle, a red 1987 Ford Thunderbird, license 897GGH, is in the garage. It is registered to the victim. It is neat and tidy.

You ask the dispatcher to check the gun through the Department of Justice records and are told the handgun in the victim's hand is registered to him. It is a Smith and Wesson revolver, Model 36, .38 caliber, serial #98246 and was registered at the time of purchase on January 10, 1987.

The Coroner's Investigator is Sam More, #235, and he arrives at 0930 hours. Investigator More, after checking the condition of the body, estimates the time of death to be within the past 10-12 hours. More adds that the death appears to be due to a self-inflicted gunshot wound. You relay the information Ramsey provided when he found the body.

Investigator More inventories the body and finds a wallet in the victim's left rear pants pocket. The wallet contains the victim's driver's license, one $5 bill, a Shell credit card, and miscellaneous photographs. A Timex watch and a silver ring were also removed from the body. These personal items are bagged and inventoried by the coroner. The coroner keeps them and gives you a copy of the inventory sheet.

Investigator More removes the gun from the victim's hand and confirms the serial number with you. The gun, ammunition box, and all ammunition are also taken by the coroner. The coroner's office has the body removed at 1130 hours. More tells you that they will attempt to locate the relatives and will notify them of the death.

Notes:

Arrestee: Jay Jodel

On today's date and time you are on patrol in a marked police car in the general vicinity of Ball Road and Walker Street.   You see Jodel walking westbound.   You see that he seems to be having difficulty walking because you see him stumble and almost fall, twice.   You stop to check on his welfare, thinking that he is either ill or drunk.   You park your car at the west curb and stop him.   You smell a strong odor of alcohol, and he admits to you that he has been drinking some beers at the local bar, the Fuzzy Bear Saloon.   You are familiar with the bar, which is about 3 blocks away.   When he speaks to you, he mumbles and you can barely understand what he is saying.   When you ask him what time it is, he tells you that it's 5:00 a.m., even though it's really 12:00 noon.   You can see that his eyes are bloodshot and watery.   His face is red and flushed.   His clothing is in poor condition, as it is dirty and it looks like he urinated in his pants.   You see what appears to be vomit on the front of his shirt.   You ask him for his driver's license and it states that he lives in Montebello.   He admits that he has no idea how he got to your city.   You conclude that he is intoxicated and is unable to care for himself, a violation of California Penal Code Section 647(f), drunk in public, and you arrest him.   You drive him to the Anaheim Police Department for booking and detention.   He is held for 4 hours and then released.

Notes:

Victim: Ralph's Food Market

Witness #1:   James Lipton

Witness #2:   Larry Earle

Suspect: Jerry Evans

You are working patrol today and are dispatched to a "shoplifter in custody" at Ralph's Food Market, 1203 West Street, Cypress. You arrive at 1930 hours. When you arrive you speak to the manager, who is witness #1, James Lipton. He takes you to his office where the suspect is being detained by another store employee, witness #2, Larry Earle. The suspect identifies himself as Jerry Evans.

Lipton tells you, "I was watching the floor from my TV monitors here in my office. I can see the entire store from here and if I see something suspicious, I let Larry know by radio and then he also keeps an eye on the person. Well, anyway, I saw this guy (he points to the suspect) walking around the store for about half an hour. This all happened about 45 minutes ago. Anyway, I noticed him because he just kept wandering around and didn't seem to be picking up anything to buy. In fact, I had Larry go up to him to see if he needed some help finding something, but he said he didn't. When Larry left the aisle the guy was in, I kept watching the guy on the monitor and saw him pick up two bottles of wine from the liquor department. I couldn't tell what kind of wine it was. He put the two bottles under his shirt and walked out of the store, never stopping to pay for the two items. I had Larry follow him outside to the front sidewalk, where I caught up to them and grabbed the guy's shirt. He dropped both bottles and they broke. The pieces of glass are still on the sidewalk. They were two bottles of Blue Nun wine and they cost $5.99. I already told him he was under arrest for theft."

You talk to Earle and he says, "I was working the floor when my boss, Jim, called me on the radio and said to watch this guy (he points to the suspect). I went up to him and asked him if he needed help. He said no. He was in the dairy products section then. I walked away and about 1 minute later my boss radioed me again that the guy had just stolen 2 bottles of wine. I saw him as he walked by at least two or three open cash registers and didn't stop to pay. I kept following him, and when we were out in front of the store, my boss caught up to us and grabbed the guy by the arm. That's when the bottles fell and broke. We brought him back here and I called you guys."

Lipton signs the private person's arrest form and tells the suspect that he has arrested him for theft. You take custody of the suspect and handcuff him. You Mirandize him but he refuses to make any statements other than to provide you his name. You search him and he has $9 in cash on him. He has no credit cards or checks on him. On the way out of the store you see the broken wine bottles. You transport him to jail for booking on the charge of petty theft, California Penal Code Section 488. He is then released on a citation, number CY348769.

126

15. PRACTICE REPORT   ARREST FOR POSSESSION OF A CONTROLLED SUBSTANCE AND A CONCEALED WEAPON

Arrestee: Cassione

You are working patrol today in a marked patrol car. You are driving southbound on Main Street, approaching 15th Street, when you see Cassione standing on the northwest corner. When you get closer, you see what appears to be a clear plastic bag in the suspect's right hand. This area is known for a high number of narcotic arrests. The suspect looks at you, quickly drops the bag on the sidewalk, and walks eastbound on 15th Street.

You immediately park your unit, get out, and pick up the bag. It is a small zip-lock sandwich bag, about 4" by 4". It contains a white powdery substance resembling cocaine. You call for another officer and you start to drive after the suspect.   You catch up to the suspect at the southwest corner of 14th Street and Main.   You arrest him for violation of Health and Safety Code Section 11350, Possession of a Controlled Substance. Your backup is Officer J. Start, #3480, and he stands by while you make the arrest and handcuff the suspect. You search the suspect and find a concealed .357 magnum, Smith and Wesson handgun in his right waistband. You charge him with violation of California Penal Code Section 12025, Possession of a Concealed Weapon.   You check him for signs of being under the influence, but he isn't. You read him his Miranda rights, but he refuses to tell you anything.   He makes no statements regarding the crime.   You handcuff him, place him in the back seat of your patrol car, and drive him to the police station.

The weapon is a stainless steel revolver with wooden grips and a 6" barrel. It's a Model 66 and the serial number is F14722. The ammunition, 6 bullets, is removed from the gun and is booked with the gun under the same evidence tag # of 12390. The contraband in the baggie is Valtox- tested **(in-the-field chemical test used by many law enforcement agencies to identify many commonly seized drugs such as cocaine, hashish, amphetamines, marijuana, methamphetamines, etc.)** and proves to be cocaine, weighing approximately 2 ounces. The cocaine is booked under evidence tag #12391.

Arrestee: John J. Doe

On today's date you are working patrol in a marked police car.   During briefing you are told by Detective R. Holt, #3489, that a felony arrest warrant, #A120987, has been issued for John J. Doe, a male Caucasian, blond hair and brown eyes, 6'-1", 170 pounds, DOB 1-23-61.   He is wanted for violation of California Penal Code Section 211, robbery.   The robbery occurred on 4-15-97 at Sunflower Liquors, 1880 W. Temple Street, Anaheim, case #9201290.   The suspect used a .38 caliber 2" chrome revolver in the robbery.   He was seen driving away from the location in a white-over-blue 2-door Chevrolet Monte Carlo, license ABC 123. The car is registered to Jane Simple of 212 N. Bendon Way, your city.   You check your department's field interrogation (FI) file and find a recent FI on Jane Simple, listing her current address as 3489 W. 3rd St., Anaheim, California.

Since Jane Simple lives in your patrol area, you and your partner, Officer Jeff Morton, #3784, decide to check her address to see if suspect John J.   Doe is there.   You and your partner drive to Jane Simple's residence; you see the car used in the robbery parked in the driveway of her residence. You draw your handgun.   You see a person matching the description of the robbery suspect run from the front yard towards the backyard. He looks directly at you and your partner and you yell "Stop! Police!" He stops. You ask him his name and he tells you that it's John J. Doe. After you confirm the suspect's name and physical description, you advise the suspect that he is under arrest for California Penal Code Section 211, Robbery, and tell him about the warrant.   Officer Morton stands by while you search the suspect.   You find a Smith and Wesson .38 caliber, 2" chrome revolver in his rear right pocket.   It is fully loaded.   You remove the gun from the suspect and unload it. You do not question the suspect nor do you advise him of his Miranda rights.

Missing Information Exercises

Complete the following 11 exercises and attempt to answer questions that are not addressed. After you have completed the report, compare your discovery with the "missing information checklist" that follows the report.

	Practice Notes
REPORT #1: ASSAULT AND BATTERY □ Follow-up Investigation DR#: 06-001 □ Supplemental Report Page 2 of 2 ■ Narrative of Incident	
INJURY Swollen left ankle of victim Virt	

On 1-11-11, at 1445 hours I was dispatched to 123 Main St. regarding an assault and battery. I arrived on scene at 1500 hours. The victim, Virt, said he was watering his front lawn when the suspect, his neighbor, Muldoon, approached him. Muldoon yelled at Virt "look you - your dog crapped all over my lawn." Virt denied that his dog had defecated on Muldoon's lawn. Muldoon went back into his residence and returned a few minutes later with a broom. Muldoon started yelling at Virt again, referring back to the dog defecating on Muldoon's lawn. While yelling he swung the broom at Virt. Virt was able to deflect the broom with his left leg and ankle area, and took the impact on his leg. Virt was struck only one time. Virt ran into his house and called police. Muldoon ran into his house after the attack.

I looked at Virt's leg and saw that it was red and starting to swell. Virt does not desire prosecution. The only witness to the attack was the victim's wife, Betty Virt. She said she had been at the kitchen window, about 35 feet from the front lawn. She couldn't hear what they were arguing about but could hear Muldoon yelling at her husband. She saw the suspect leave and return with a broom. She saw the suspect hit her husband's left leg with the broom.

Both the victim and his wife know the suspect as their neighbor and gave me his name and address.

Muldoon said he believed that Virt's dog had defecated on his lawn and he admitted to the attack. Muldoon apologized for the incident and explained that he had just lost his job and was upset about finding feces on his lawn. Muldoon said he would not repeat the incident.

List the Missing information:

DR#: <u>06-001</u>

MISSING INFORMATION:

1.   The phrase "a few minutes" (line 8) is not specific enough; obtain an approximate time.

2.   You should offer medical aid. If victim refuses, state this in the report.

3.   Has the victim ever experienced any other problems with the neighbor?

4.   Was the victim struck by the broomstick or by the brush portion of the broom?

5.   How does the victim know his dog was not involved (i.e., had not defecated on the lawn)?

☐ Follow-up Investigation   DR#: <u>06-002</u>

<u>INJURY</u>

Bruised right eye of victim Bowers (photo attached)

On 1-11-11, at 1930 hours I was dispatched to 123 Main St. regarding a domestic dispute.   I arrived on scene at 1945 hours. The follow-up officer, Smith, #212, arrived at 1946 hours. While I talked to the victim, Officer Smith stood-by with the suspect.

The victim, Sally Bowers, said she had arrived home at about 1915 hours and found that her husband, the suspect, Marvin Bowers, had been drinking. He was in a bad mood and when she asked him what was wrong he told her he had been fired from his job.   Sally said she wasn't surprised because he drinks too much.   He got angry at her and when she turned to walk away he grabbed her arm and spun her around. He slapped her on the face knocking her to the floor. She went into the bathroom and saw bruising begin to form, creating a black right eye. She said "I called you because I'm tired of him beating up on me—this is not the first time, you know, but I'm afraid of him. I don't want him arrested—that'll only make things worse."

The victim refused any medical aid. I could see the start of a black and blue right eye. I took a photo of the eye. I gave the victim the Domestic Violence form, #209, which provided the victim with information on shelters, counseling, and the right to make an arrest.

I read the Miranda advisement to the suspect and he said "She had no business calling you guys- I told her I was fired and she started calling me names and a 'drunk'. I never hit her- she hit her face on the door when she stormed out of the room. She's a bitch and she's always bitching about something and calling me names. She can go to hell; I'm going to file for divorce."

I arrested the suspect and charged him with violation of California Penal Code Section 273.5, Spousal Abuse.

List the Missing information:

DR#: 06-002

MISSING INFORMATION:

1.   The victim says that the husband had been drinking. What caused her to come to this conclusion?

2.   Did you smell alcohol on the suspect?   Was he drunk?   Was there evidence (bottles, etc.) of an alcoholic beverage? Was there other evidence that a fight had taken place, such as table or chair overturned ?

3.   Which of the victim's arms did the suspect grab?

4.   What was the disposition of the suspect? Was he booked at your jail or did he bail out?

5.   Is there a history of the victim and suspect having previous similar incidents?
            If so, what were they?

6.   Were there children present while the domestic violence was in progress? If the children were present, were they interviewed, removed from the home, etc.?

7.   Is the victim willing to prosecute?

8.   Are there any weapons in the house, in particular, guns that could be legally removed for safekeeping, and for the victim's future safety?

PROPERTY LOSS

$100 Cash	U.S. currency; miscellaneous bills (victim #1/Due)	$100.00
$ 25 Cash	U.S. currency, miscellaneous bills (victim #2/Downs)	$ 25.00

1 - leather handbag and contents: brush, comb, pack of cigarettes, gold cigarette
lighter (recovered and returned to victim #2/Downs)

Total Combined Loss	$125.00

EVIDENCE
1 - Twine   Tag # 12390
1 - Tape   Tag # 12391

She said   she was not injured.   She thought the crime occurred about 10 minutes before she called the police. She did not hear any cars drive from the area. She didn't think that she would be able to recognize the suspect if she saw him again. She provided the description of the suspect that appears on page 1 of this report. She said the suspect seemed very calm.

She could not provide much information about the suspect's gun because she is not familiar with handguns. She saw that the gun was chrome but didn't know if it was a revolver or semi-automatic or how big it was. She thought the suspect may have touched the outside of the bathroom door around the doorknob and also the cashier's counter top. The suspect did not wear gloves.

She said that just before I arrived, she discovered that her purse had been stolen. She had left the purse behind the counter on the floor, and now the purse was gone.

The reporting party, Moody, said he drove into the gas station to get gas and went into the station to give the cashier his credit card. He waited for a couple of minutes and no one appeared.   He yelled out "anyone here?" and that was when he heard the victim kicking the bathroom door. He opened the bathroom door, saw that she had been tied up, and freed her. He did not see anyone else in or around the area of the gas station at anytime.

I walked through the business with Downs and she showed me where the tape and twine had been left on the bathroom floor. I collected both the twine and tape and later booked them into evidence. I walked outside to look for evidence, and while looking through a trash can I found the victim's purse. After she verified that all the contents except the cash were still there, the purse and contents were returned to her.

I requested a crime scene investigator and Officer Robin arrived to handle collecting fingerprints. He will have a supplemental report.

Both the victims are willing to prosecute.

List the Missing information:

DR#: 06-003

MISSING INFORMATION:

Introduction

There is no introduction to this report. Was the officer dispatched to the incident or did he/she observe the activity? What is the time of arrival and who did he/she contact?

1. Promptly provide dispatch with the suspect's description, weapon, and loss, for a crime broadcast.

2. Provide a description of the store, such as square footage, alarms, doors, windows, etc.

3. Is there a video camera in the store?

4. Were there any customers in the station just before the robbery? If there were, and if they charged gas, etc., they should be located through the charge receipts and interviewed, in case they saw the suspect.

5. The cashier doesn't seem to think she could recognize the suspect if she saw him again, yet she provided a good description of him. Can she tell you what makes her think she couldn't recognize him? Was she afraid of him?

6. What does she mean when she says the suspect was calm? Be specific.

7. She can't provide much information on the suspect's gun. Use your own gun for comparison purposes to get a better weapon description.

8. Did she check the rest of the station for additional losses?

9. Did the reporting party touch anything?

REPORT #4: ROBBERY, BURGLARY, AND ASSAULT WITH A DEADLY WEAPON

PROPERTY LOSS

$2,500 cash, U.S. currency, miscellaneous bills $2,500.00

On 1-11-11 at 0745 hours I was dispatched to Lucky Supermarket at 123 Main St., regarding a robbery report. I arrived on scene at 0755 hours. The victim, Byers, told me she is the manager of the store. She arrived this morning at about 0730 hours. The store opens at 0800 hours. Other employees also usually start to arrive at 0730. She entered through the front doors. She locked the doors behind her and turned off the alarm. She said that she noticed nothing out of place. She walked to the back of the store where her office is and where the safe is located. She heard a noise behind her and when she turned around she saw the suspect holding a knife and pointing it at her. He told her to hurry and open up the safe. She recalled exactly what the suspect said. It was "Hurry up, bitch, and open the safe." She said the suspect seemed very nervous because he was sweating and the hand holding the knife was shaking. While she was opening the safe she heard someone knocking on the front doors, and she knew it had to be an employee. She handed the cash to the suspect and he put it in his left front jacket pocket. The suspect had also heard the knocking and yelled at her to find another way for him to get out.

The store is located in a commercial complex and is a single story building. There are neighboring businesses on each side of the building and an alley that runs behind the store. The alley borders the railroad tracks. The store has one set of double front doors that are locked with a dead bolt lock. The deadbolt requires a key to lock and unlock from the inside or the outside. I saw that the rear door still had a horizontal bar in place and it was locked with a combination lock. All the doors and windows are connected to the alarm, which is a burglar alarm only. The alarm is monitored through WestPac Alarms.

The back office door was still locked, with a bar in place, so she started to unlock it so he could get out that way. But as she was doing that, he grabbed her and started pulling her towards the front door, all the time holding the knife close to her throat. He kept saying to her, over and over, "Don't give me a reason to cut your throat, lady. I will, I got nothin' to lose." She saw the witness, Smit, standing at the door. Smit saw the suspect and she started to scream. The suspect yelled at her to 'shut up' and told Byers to unlock the front doors. She did, and the suspect ran southbound on Salton Sea. She did not see where he ran from there. Byers said that she was scared but unhurt. She is confident that she would be able to recognize the suspect and wants to prosecute.

Byers said that she had no idea how the suspect entered the store, because he was already there when she entered. She could only estimate the monetary loss at the time of this report. She said by examining the previous night's receipts she could better estimate the loss. She gave the description of the suspect and it appears on page 1 of this report. She added that the suspect had a slight limp.

I broadcasted the suspect's description that the weapon was a knife, the estimated loss, and the suspect's direction of travel to nearby police officers but they were unable to locate any probable suspect.

The witness, Smit, said that she didn't know anyone else was in the store with Byers because she only saw Byers' car in the parking lot. When Smit got to the front doors and knocked, she saw the suspect holding a knife at Byers' throat. Smit thought that she probably started to scream, at which point the suspect started to yell and Byers tried to open the front door with her keys. Once Byers opened the door, the suspect pushed past Smit. Smit said, "I got a real good look at his face. I would know him anywhere." Smit described the suspect as a male Hispanic, about 25 years old, black hair, 5"-7" to 5"-9" tall, 150-160 pounds, wearing a white t-shirt and black pants.

Byers escorted me on a tour of the building so I could determine how the suspect got into the store. We walked into the warehouse located at the rear of the store. I saw that a roof vent cover had been removed. I saw several boxes stacked on top of one another, which would allow someone to climb up to or down from the roof vent. Byers said the vent cover is never off and that it wasn't like that when she closed the store the night before at

2300 hours. She said that every night before she leaves she takes a tour of the building just to make sure that all employees and patrons are gone. She said she would've noticed the stacked boxes and removed vent cover. She didn't believe the vent was connected to the alarm system.

I called for a crime scene investigator and Officer Brown arrived to handle the collection of evidence. He will write a separate report.

List the Missing information

DR#: 06-004

MISSING INFORMATION:

1.   Are there cameras in the store?

2.   The victim states that she heard a noise that caused her to turn around and discover the suspect. Go into greater detail. What was the noise?

3.   Get a description of the knife.

4.   Which leg had the limp?

5.   Provide the time of your crime broadcast.

6.   You should gain access to the roof to check for evidence and verify if the vent cover is connected to the alarm system.

7.   Call the alarm company to find out if there had been any alarm activations during the time the store was closed and prior to the time the crime was committed.

Notes:

INJURIES

One gunshot wound in victim's upper left thigh.

On 1-11-11, at 1815 hours I was dispatched to 123 Main St. regarding an assault with a deadly weapon investigation at Albertson's Food Market. I arrived on scene and was met by both witnesses. The victim, Smythe, was lying down. I saw that his upper left thigh was bleeding from what appeared to be a gunshot wound. The paramedics told me the victim's injury was not life-threatening, so they allowed me to talk to him.

The victim said that he and his roommate, witness #1, Stanley, were at the market doing their weekly grocery shopping. After they were inside the store, Smythe realized that he had left his wallet in the glove compartment of his car. Smythe returned to his car and Stanley stayed inside the store to shop. When Smythe reached his car, he saw the suspect inside it. It appeared that the suspect was trying to start the car. Smythe walked up to his car and yelled at the suspect to get out of his car. The suspect jumped out of the car from the driver's side; Smythe tried to grab onto him to stop him. The two of them fell to the ground, punching each other. Suddenly, and without any warning, the suspect pulled a gun out from a pocket of the jacket he was wearing, pointed the gun at Smythe and fired it. The bullet hit Smythe in the thigh. Smythe said the suspect fled on foot westbound through the parking lot and then westbound onto Ward Street.

Smythe gave the description of the suspect that appears on page 1 of this report. He described the suspect's gun as a chrome revolver, possibly a "4-inch" revolver. Smythe said that he would recognize the suspect if he saw him again and will prosecute. I broadcasted the suspect's description, weapon and direction of travel to other nearby police units

Witness #1, Stanley, said he was wondering what was taking Smythe so long just to get his wallet. As Stanley walked outside, he heard a shot and saw Smythe on the ground. Stanley did not see the suspect and Smythe struggling on the ground. As Stanley ran toward Smythe, he saw the suspect run westbound on Ward St. Stanley said he would be able to recognize the suspect if he saw him again. Stanley could only describe the suspect's gun as a chrome revolver. Stanley said the description provided by Smythe was correct, but he added that he thought the suspect had been wearing a green baseball hat with white unknown lettering on the front of the hat.

Witness #2, Jaclin, said he was in the parking lot loading up his truck when he saw the suspect and Smythe struggling on the ground. Jaclin started to run to Smythe's aid and heard the shot. He saw the suspect run away, westbound on Ward Street. He said the suspect was a male Hispanic, about 20-25 years old, 5' 7" to 5'10", about 150-175 pounds, black hair and unknown eye color.

I inspected Smythe's vehicle, which was parked on the east side of the market. The vehicle, an all black 1993 Cadillac El Dorado STS, license plate CLASIC, is registered to Smythe. I saw that the driver's window was broken and the ignition had been pulled from the steering column. I saw a screwdriver on the floor of the car near the accelerator pedal. I saw the glove compartment was open and I looked for Smythe's wallet, but it was not there.

Paramedic Winchell, #346, said the victim had a through-and-through gunshot wound of the thigh and would require additional medical attention. Before the ambulance took Smythe to the hospital, I asked him if the screwdriver was his and he said it wasn't. Smythe said the car had been locked and all of the windows had been rolled up. Medix ambulance took Smythe to Huntington Beach Memorial Hospital at 12398 Lakeshore Drive, Huntington Beach.

I requested a crime scene investigator to take photos of the vehicle and to collect all evidence.

List the Missing information

DR#: <u>06-05</u>

<u>MISSING INFORMATION:</u>

1.   What was your arrival time at the scene?

2.   Where did you find the victim when you got to Albertson's? In the parking lot?

3.   When the victim walked up to the suspect and yelled at him, what did the victim say?

4.   Did the suspect make a statement?

5.   Does witness #2, Jaclin, recall seeing the gun? Can he describe it?

6.   What time did you make the broadcast? Was a suspect ever located?

7.   What is the name of the crime scene investigator who handled the evidence?

8.   What was the disposition of the victim's vehicle? Towed? Given to roommate?

9.   What time did the ambulance take the victim from the crime scene to the hospital?

10.   Before you left the scene, did you search the parking lot for other witnesses?

On 1-11-11, at 1430 hours I was dispatched to 123 Main St. regarding an attempted suicide. While en route, dispatch said the reporting party was a hot-line volunteer, Ken Mathis, of United Churches Suicide Hot Line in Anaheim. Mathis told dispatch that Marion David called the hotline and told him that she was going to kill herself with sleeping pills. Mathis kept David on the line long enough for the call to be traced to the address that dispatch had sent me to.

I arrived at 0930 hours and my follow-up officer, Officer S. Parker, #3645, arrived at about 0931 hours. We knocked on the front door of the residence and David came to the door and let us in. She said she was extremely depressed and she had been talking with someone on suicide hot-line. The phone was still off the hook and Mathis was still on the line. While Officer Parker stayed with David, I talked to Mathis, who confirmed the information that dispatch had previously given me.

David told me she was depressed because her father had died in a boating accident two days ago in San Francisco. She said her father had been her only living relative and she had no one locally who cared about her. Her old boyfriend, Sam Horner, and she had broken up about two months ago when she caught him with an old girlfriend. David said she had been seeing a psychiatrist for depression and had been taking two medications. Her doctor is Dr. Jerry Bump, phone # 310-388-9990. She admitted to swallowing all the pills from the two medication bottles. I looked at the bottles left on the counter in the kitchen and both were empty. One bottle was marked 'Valium' and the other was marked 'Paxil.'

I requested that paramedics be sent. Once they arrived, they treated David for ingestion of the pills. David had now become incoherent, possibly as a result of medication. She started to mumble and could not tell me anything else.

The paramedics took David to Charter Hospital, 2233 N. Lemon St., for further treatment. Dr. Jake Hall pumped her stomach. He said that due to the circumstances, he would admit her to the hospital for mental evaluation by the hospital's psychiatric staff.

I completed the Welfare and Institutions Code Section 5150 form stating that I considered David a danger to herself and left her in the custody of Dr. Hall.

List the Missing information

DR#: 06-06

MISSING INFORMATION:

1.   Was there anyone else in the house? Did you check? Does anyone else live there with her?

2.   Has she attempted suicide before?

3.   Did you look for other medications, etc., that she could've ingested?

4.   You should take the medication bottles with you or give them to the paramedics.   Were the medication bottles in her name?

5.   What were the names of the paramedics who treated her? What time did they take her to the hospital?

6.   Did you call her psychiatrist? Did you tell Dr. Hall who her psychiatrist is?

On 1-11-11, at 0725 I was dispatched to 123 Main St. regarding a possible suicide. When the paramedics and I arrived at 0740 hours, the witness, Ramsey, was standing outside the victim's residence. Ramsey pointed to the house and said the victim, Bothom, was inside. Officer Smith, #234, and I checked the residence for additional people; there were none. We secured the residence. I looked at Bothom and saw a bloody wound in his left temple. I also saw a handgun in his left hand. I checked Bothom for signs of life and found none. Orange County Fire Authority, Engine #16, Station 21, Paramedics J. Dixon, #23, and M. De Gaulle, #298, pronounced Bothom dead at 0744 hours. At 0744 hours, I requested a deputy coroner be sent to the scene.

Ramsey said that he had known Bothom, his next-door neighbor, for about 5 years. The two of them had made arrangements to go golfing today. Ramsey said he telephoned Bothom at about 0715 hours and when he didn't answer he went next door. When he knocked on the victim's front door, there was no answer. He tried the doorknob; the door was unlocked. He walked into the living room and found Bothom on the floor. Ramsey said that when he saw Bothom's bloody head and the gun in Bothom's hand, he thought Bothom was dead. Ramsey said that he touched nothing and called the police from Bothom's kitchen phone.

Ramsey said he and Bothom had talked the night before at about 1800 hours. They confirmed their golf date. Ramsey said he lives next door and heard nothing unusual during the night. He hadn't seen anyone at the residence other than the victim. Ramsey had no knowledge of anyone else living at the residence with the victim. Ramsey could not explain why Bothom would kill himself. He did say that Bothom had been out of work for about 8 months. Ramsey does not know if Bothom had any relatives, a girlfriend, etc.

While waiting for the deputy coroner to arrive, I saw that Bothom's body was beginning to stiffen and blood had coagulated on his left temple and onto the floor. I saw what appeared to be deposits of black powder on the temple, surrounding the entry wound. Bothom was lying on his back, with his head facing northeast. The handgun was still in Bothom's left hand and his finger was still around the trigger. I saw splatters of blood on the handgun. The victim was fully clothed in a pair of blue Levi's, a white T-shirt, tennis shoes, and socks. I saw blood on the T-shirt. I saw no injuries to the body other than the head wound.

I saw, on a nearby coffee table, an opened box of .38 caliber ammunition. Next to it was a leather handgun carrying case.

I checked the house and it was tidy and clean. Nothing appeared out of order. I could not find a suicide note. The house is single story, with three bedrooms, a kitchen, and two bathrooms; there is an unattached garage. The vehicle, a red 1987 Ford Thunderbird, license 897GGH, was parked in the garage. It is registered to Bothom. The car was neat and tidy.

Deputy Coroner S. More, Badge #235, arrived at 0930 hours. I told him what Ramsey told me when he found the body. More estimated the time of death to be within the past 10-16 hours and added that the injury appeared to be a self-inflicted gunshot wound.

More removed the gun from Bothom's hand and confirmed the serial number. Upon checking with the Department of Justice records, I learned the gun was registered to Bothom and had been registered at time of purchase, which was 1-10-87. The gun was a Smith and Wesson Model 36, .38 caliber, serial #98246. The gun, ammunition box, and all ammunition were taken by More.

More inventoried the body and found a wallet in the left rear pants pocket. The wallet contained Bothom's driver's license, one $5 bill, a Shell credit card, and miscellaneous photographs. More also removed a Timex watch and a silver ring from the body. All of these items were bagged and inventoried by More. More gave me a copy of the inventory and he took all of the personal items.

At the request of More, the body was removed at 1130 hours. More said his office would attempt to locate the relatives to notify them of the death.

List the Missing information

DR#: <u>06-07</u>

<u>**MISSING INFORMATION:**</u>

1.   You say you checked for signs of life. What does that mean?

2.   Did the witness know of previous suicide attempts?

3.   Can other neighbors provide any information?

4.   What part(s) of the body were beginning to stiffen? Did you see any discoloration on the body?

5.   Was the gun loaded? Had it been fired? How many times? Was it a revolver or automatic? If automatic, there should be expended shell casings.

6.   Were the lights still on? Messages on the answering machine?

7.   Would there be an autopsy? When would the results be known?

8.   What was the disposition of the residence? Did the victim rent or own the residence?

143

REPORT #8:   DRUNK IN PUBLIC ARREST

On 1-11-11, I was on patrol in a marked police car in the vicinity of Ball Road and Walker Street.   I saw the suspect, Jodel, walking westbound.   I saw that he appeared to have difficulty walking because he stumbled and almost fell, twice. I stopped my police car, parked it at the west curb, got out and walked toward the suspect, intending to check on his welfare, thinking he was either ill or drunk. When I got next to the suspect, I smelled a strong odor of alcohol; the suspect admitted to me that he had been drinking some beers at the local bar, the Fuzzy Bear Saloon.   I am familiar with the bar, which is about 3 blocks away. When Jodel spoke to me, he mumbled his words so much that I could barely understand what he was saying.   When I asked Jodel what time it was, he said the time was 0500 hours. In fact, the time was 1200 hours. I saw that Jodel's eyes were watery and bloodshot.   His face was red and flushed.   His clothing was dirty and it appeared that he had urinated in his pants. I saw what appeared to be vomit on the front of his shirt. I asked him for his driver's license. According to the license, he lived in Montebello.   He had no idea how he had arrived in Anaheim.   I concluded that he was intoxicated and unable to care for himself, a violation of California Penal Code Section 647 (f), drunk in public, and I arrested him.

Jodel was booked at the Anaheim city jail. He was released after remaining in detention for four hours.

DR#: 06-08 MISSING INFORMATION:

None.

144

PROPERTY LOSS

2 - broken bottles of Blue Nun wine @ $5. 99 each $11.98

On 1-11-11, at 1910 hours I was dispatched to a "shoplifter in custody" at Ralph's food market. I arrived on scene at 1930 hours and spoke with the manager, witness #1, Lipton. He took me to his office where the suspect was being detained by another store employee, witness #2, Earle. The suspect had identified himself as Jerry Evans.

Lipton said he had been watching the "floor" (shopping area) on the TV monitors in his office. Whenever he sees someone suspicious, he radios to Earle, who then also monitors the person. Lipton said that, via the monitors, he watched Evans walking around inside the store for about half an hour without picking up anything to examine or possibly buy. Lipton told Earle to help Evans but Evans told Earle he didn't need any help. After Earle left Evans, Lipton continued to watch Evans and saw him pick up two bottles of wine from a shelf in the liquor department. Lipton could not identify the type of wine it was.   Evans put the wine bottles under his shirt and walked out of the store, never stopping to pay for the items. Earle followed Evans outside where Lipton caught up to them. Lipton grabbed Evans by the arm, and when he did so, the bottles Evans had under his shirt fell to the ground and broke. Lipton said the broken bottles were still on the sidewalk.   Lipton, prior to my arrival, told Evans he was under arrest for theft.

Earle said he was told by Lipton via radio to watch Evans. Earle asked Evans if he needed help and Evans said he didn't. At that point, Evans was in the dairy section. Earle walked away, and about 1 minute later Lipton radioed to him that Evans had just stolen two bottles of wine.   Earle saw Evans walk past two or three open check-out stations; Evans did not stop to pay for the wine. Earle followed Evans out of the store. When they were outside, Lipton caught up to them, and when Lipton grabbed Evans' arm, the bottles fell and broke.   Evans was brought back to the office and the police were called.

Lipton signed the private person's arrest form and told Evans he had been arrested for theft. I handcuffed Evans. I Mirandized Evans, but he refused to make any statements other than to give me his name, date of birth, and address. I searched him and found $9.00 in cash on him. Evans had no credit cards or checks on him.

While I was escorting Evans out of the store to my police car, I saw the broken wine bottles on the ground in front of the store.

I drove Evans to the jail for booking on the charge of petty theft, California Penal Code Section 488. Evans was then released on citation, # CY348769.

Missing Information:

DR#: <u>06-09</u>

<u>MISSING INFORMATION:</u>

1. Is the activity viewed on the TV monitors tape recorded? If so, you will need the tape as evidence. You should watch the tape and write in the report what you saw.

2. Although the suspect was Mirandized and refused to talk about the charge against him, what was his exact statement of refusal?

3. Has either of the witnesses seen Evans in the store before? If so, what did he do on that/those occasion(s)?

Notes

REPORT #10: POSSESSION OF WEAPON AND DRUGS	

EVIDENCE

1 - 4" by 4" zip lock sandwich bag containing 2 ounces of a white powdery substance   Tag # 12391

2 - Smith and Wesson .357 handgun, model 177, serial number #F14722, stainless
   steel revolver, wooden grips, 6" barrel; 6 bullets that were used

On 1-11-11, at 1300 hours I was working patrol in a marked police car. I am familiar with this area as having a high number of narcotic arrests. I was driving southbound on Main Street, approaching 15th Street, when I saw the suspect, Cassione, standing on the northwest corner. As I got closer to Cassione, I saw what appeared to be a clear plastic bag in his right hand. Cassione looked in my direction, dropped the bag on the sidewalk and started walking eastbound on 15th Street.

I parked my car, got out, and picked up the bag. I saw that it was a zip-lock sandwich bag measuring about 4 inches by 4 inches. I saw that it contained a white powdery substance resembling cocaine. I radioed for another officer and started to drive after Cassione.

I caught up to Cassione at 14th Street and Main. Officer J. Start, #3480, was the backup officer and he stood by while I arrested Cassione and handcuffed him. I arrested him for violation of Health and Safety Code Section 11350, Possession of a Controlled Substance. I searched him and found a concealed handgun in his right waistband, a violation of California Penal Code Section 12025, Possession of a Concealed Weapon. The gun was loaded with six bullets; I unloaded it. I checked Cassione for being under the influence of drugs; he wasn't. I read him his Miranda rights, but he refused to make any statements. Having arrested Cassione for the violations, I transported him to the police station. Once there, I Valtox-tested the contents of the bag; the substance proved to be cocaine.

Missing information

DR #: <u>06-010</u>

<u>**MISSING INFORMATION:**</u>

1. Explain in detail how you know this is an area having a high number of narcotic arrests. If you've made arrests in this area for similar offenses, say so. If your narcotic detectives have provided arrest information, say so.

2. Give an approximate distance between you and Cassione at the time you first saw him. Give an approximate distance between you and Cassione when you saw the baggie in his hand.

3. Expand on the distance traveled until you caught up with the suspect (number of feet, blocks, etc.)

4. What is the suspect's disposition? Held for bail, cited out?

On 1-11-11, Detective Holt, #3489, advised me that an arrest warrant, #A120987, had been issued for John J. Doe, a male Caucasian, with blond hair and brown eyes, height 6'1", weight 170 pounds, date of birth: January 23,1961.   The warrant was for violation of California Penal Code Section 211, Robbery. The robbery had occurred on April 15, 1997 at Sunflower Liquors, 1880 W. Temple Street, Anaheim, Case #9201290. The suspect used a .38 caliber 2" chrome revolver in the robbery. Doe was seen driving away from the location in a white-over-blue 2-door 1985 Chevrolet Monte Carlo, license ABC 123.   The car is currently registered to Jan Simple of 212 N. Bendon Way, Anaheim.

Prior to going on patrol I checked the department's field interrogation file (FI) and found a recent FI on Jane Simple, listing her current address as 3489 W. 3rd St., Anaheim.

Since Simple's address was in my patrol area, my partner, Officer Jeff Morton, #3784, and I decided to check the address to see if the suspect Doe was there. We arrived at the location at 1944 hours and I saw parked in the driveway of the residence the car that had been used in the robbery. I drew my handgun.   I saw a male matching the description of the robbery suspect run from the front yard towards the backyard. The male looked at me and my partner and I yelled "Stop!" "Police!"   He stopped. I asked him his name and he told me it was John J. Doe. I confirmed his name and physical description and advised him that he was under arrest for California Penal Code Section 211, Robbery.   I told him about the warrant. Officer Morton stood by while I searched Doe. In the left rear pocket I found a fully loaded Smith and Wesson .38 caliber, 2" chrome-plated revolver. I removed the gun and unloaded it. I did not question Doe or advise him of his Miranda rights.

We drove Doe to the jail for booking on the warrant and notified Detective Holt.   Holt said he would interview the suspect. When Holt arrived he took possession of the gun and ammunition.

Missing information

Blank page for notes:

Narrative exercises:

To excel in report writing, rewrite the following narratives several times. It will help you develop a systematic approach to situations. Your instructor will adjust or add specific verbiage unique to each individual agency as necessary.

Narrative #1 - Mentally ill person

PROPERTY:

1 - Machete with red handle.   Tag #283674

On 1-11-11, at approximately 1100 hours I was on foot patrol in the area of Morris Park.   At briefing earlier this date Sergeant Donell said that several citizen complaints had been received regarding vagrants living in the park.   The vagrants had accosted and harassed citizens who were using the park facilities.

While I was walking along the west parkway I saw Miles talking to an unknown male.   The male motioned with his hand for me to come to him.   He told me that he felt that Miles was a danger to the public because he had a machete that he was waving around and he did not seem to be coherent.   I requested another officer to assist me, and Officer Ertin was dispatched to my location.   I asked the unknown male to remain at the scene so I could obtain further information, but he refused to stay and left the area.

I saw the machete on a park bench, about 5-7 feet from where Miles was standing.   I started to talk to Miles and quickly formed the opinion that he was possibly mentally ill.   He did not seem to know where he was or what day it was, and much of his speech was slurred and incoherent.   He told me that he had tried to kill himself several months ago.   After he told me about the attempted suicide, his speech became incoherent again and I couldn't get any further information from him.   He made several statements that caused me to be concerned for citizens using the park.   He claimed the park was his and he knew he had to "rid the park of the beasts who destroy it."   He also said he had already "eliminated the undesirables" but would not go further into what he meant.   Once again he became incoherent.   While he was talking, he frequently hit his face with his fist and shouted incoherent phrases at passersby.

Miles" appearance was unkempt.   He smelled of body odor and his clothes were dirty and sour-smelling.   His hair and beard were matted and dirty.   Although he was wearing a shoe and sock on his right foot, his left foot was bare, and I didn't see any shoes or socks in the immediate viewing area.

Once Officer Ertin arrived I took Miles into custody under the authority of Welfare and Institutions Code Section 5150 as a Danger to Others.

When I attempted to handcuff Miles, he became violent to such a degree that both Officer Ertin and I had to push him to the ground in an attempt to place his arms behind his back. He kicked at me and was yelling "I'm God," and "You'll pay in hell." Neither Miles, nor Officer Ertin or I were injured in the fight. I took the machete and booked it under tag # 283674, for destruction. I drove Miles to Charter Hospital, 12687 Cherry Avenue in Long Beach for 72-hour observation.

Case closed.

Narrative #2 - Theft

On 1-11-11, at 1610 hours I was dispatched to the 123 Main St. regarding a theft. When I arrived at 1625 hours, the victim, Delroy, told me the following: he had parked his vehicle, a 1989 Jeep Cherokee, California license Y345OPO, in his driveway at 1545 hours. He left the TV and phone on the backseat of the vehicle and left the cash in the glove compartment. The vehicle's driver's side window was rolled down and the driver's side door was left unlocked.

Delroy said he had not intended to be inside his house so long. He lost track of time. About 30 minutes after he went into the house, he remembered that the items were in the vehicle and the window was down and the door was unlocked. When he returned to the vehicle at about 1615 hours he discovered the items were gone. He did not see or hear anything unusual. Delroy had no idea who might've committed the theft and said he would support prosecution if the suspect was located.

Before I left the area I went to the following addresses in an attempt to locate witnesses: 4356, 4357, 4358, 4359 Oakdale. No one came to the door at any of the addresses, so I left my business card with a note requesting the resident at each address to call me.

Case closed pending additional information.

Narrative #2a - Residential burglary

On 1-11-11, at 1130 hours I was on patrol in a marked patrol car in the area of 6000 Leaf Drive when the victim, Brown, flagged me down. He told me that he had just arrived home and discovered that his house had been broken into. He showed me the house, which is a 1-story stucco building with three bedrooms, kitchen, den, and two baths, with an attached two-car garage. The house has no alarm. The address is 6000 Leaf Drive.

Brown said he had arrived home at about 1000 hours from a three-day vacation. After driving into his garage he noticed the door that leads into the house from the garage interior was splintered and leaning against the garage doorframe. He walked into the house and discovered it had been burglarized.

Brown took me on a tour of the house and showed me the desk in the den where the television and laptop computer had been when he went on vacation. I could see an outline of dust on the desk and I could see where two rectangular items had rested. Brown took me on a room-by-room tour; it seemed that the rest of the house had not been disturbed.

Brown said he lived in the house by himself and no one had permission to be in the house other than his neighbor, James Blount, (DOB 2-4-43), 5800 Leaf Drive, (714) 555-1111. Mr. Blount had keys to the house and would check on the house for the victim whenever the victim was gone. Brown said he had no idea who might've committed the burglary and said he would support prosecution if the suspect is found.

Narrative #3 - Commercial robbery

PROPERTY LOSS $250 cash, U.S. currency, miscellaneous bills

EVIDENCE   1 - Videotape of robbery Tag # 23980

On 1-11-11, at 2230 hours I was dispatched to the Sav-On Drugstore at 1278 N. Brookhurst regarding a robbery that had just occurred. While en route, I was given the description of the two suspects, their vehicle, and direction of travel. That information appears on the front page of this report.

I arrived at 2235 hours and spoke with the victim, Brown. I confirmed the suspect and vehicle descriptions I had previously been given, and confirmed that both suspects were armed with handguns. Brown said the robbery occurred about 5 minutes before I arrived.

I requested that dispatch advise Orange County Communications of the robbery and that a general broadcast be made alerting all Orange County law enforcement agencies to the suspect and vehicle descriptions. That broadcast was made at 2245 hours, broadcast #22-458-23.

Brown told me he had been working behind the photo counter at about 2230 hours. He was in the process of closing his cash register and was counting the money on the counter. To the best of his knowledge there were no customers in the store. The only other employee was Smith. Brown looked up to see the two suspects enter the north doors and immediately walk to the photo counter. He said he had never seen the two suspects before but felt threatened because they were wearing bulky clothing and both looked at the cash on the counter. He said that as the suspects approached the counter they took guns out from underneath their bulky jackets and pointed the guns at him.

Suspect #1 said to him, "Give me all the money or I'll blow your damn head off." Suspect #2 never said anything. Brown said both suspects appeared to be nervous because their foreheads were sweating and their handguns shook. Brown said, "I was so scared—I thought for sure they would shoot me." He handed all the money on the counter to suspect #1 and the two suspects ran out the north doors and in an unknown direction from there. Brown then called the police.

Brown said he had enough time as the suspects approached the counter to push the auto-record button to the closed-circuit camera to capture the robbery on tape. I watched the videotape and because it was in color I could see the suspects' clothing description, etc., provided by Brown appeared to be accurate. He gave me the tape and I booked it into evidence. He said the suspects did not touch the counter top. Brown said he is experienced with handguns and he believed the guns were .38 caliber blue-steel revolvers with 4" barrels. Brown said he would recognize both suspects if he saw them again and would support prosecution.

Witness Smith told me that at the time the robbery occurred, she had been standing near the pharmacy, about 35 feet away from the photo counter where Brown had been counting the money. She saw the two suspects enter through the north doors and thought it was strange that the two were wearing such heavy, bulky clothing because the weather was so hot. She did not think that either suspect saw her since she was partially hidden by the pharmacy counter. She watched as the suspects walked to the photo counter and pulled out their guns. She saw the suspects point the guns at Brown but could not hear what the suspects said to Brown. She did not see their faces and only saw the suspects from the rear. She did not think she could recognize the suspects if she saw them again. The description she provided of the suspects' clothing matched the description the victim had given me and the information matched what I saw on the video tape, but she added that the suspect who did all the talking (suspect #1) was wearing a gold earring in his left earlobe.

Witness Smith said that after the suspects left the store through the north doors, she looked around the corner to see the suspects get into the vehicle described on page 1. She provided the description of the suspect vehicle but was unable to see a rear license plate because the lighting was poor. She said suspect #2 drove the vehicle north on Brookhurst and then was out of sight. She would be able to recognize the vehicle if she saw it again and would testify. Case closed pending review by detectives.

Narrative #4 - Domestic violence

INJURIES   *Blackened right eye and cheek of victim (photo attached)*
Tag # 19728

On 1-11-11, at 2345 hours I was dispatched to 123 Main St. regarding a fight between husband and wife. Officer Erin was the assigned follow-up officer. When I arrived the victim, M. Brown, met me at the front door of the residence. She said she had called the police because her husband, E. Brown, had struck her in the face with his hand. While Officer Erin talked to the suspect, I spoke with the victim.

The victim told me that she had arrived home from work at about 1640 hours. She immediately discovered that her husband had not gone to work today but had stayed home and had apparently been drinking. She believed that he had been drinking because he smelled of alcohol and there were several empty beer cans strewn about the living room. When she went into the living room, she saw her husband sleeping on the couch. She woke him up and he immediately got mad at her for doing so.

She said he called her a "bitch" and hit her with an open hand on the right side of her face. She said he had pushed her before but had never struck her like he did today. She said she did nothing to provoke the injury. She refused medical aid. She said she wanted him arrested and would testify.

I could see swelling and black-and-blue bruising on the right side of her face. Her right eyelid and the skin under the eye had already started to turn black-and-blue. I took a Polaroid photo of the injury and that photo is included with this report.

I looked into the living room and saw several chairs, tables, and knickknacks strewn about in disarray, which gave me the impression that a fight may have occurred. There were five empty Budweiser beer cans on the living room floor.

I read E. Brown the Miranda Advisement, Form #347. He said, "Yeah, I'll tell ya what happened," and signed the form waiving his rights. He agreed with the statement of the victim, up to the point where the victim said she had received her injuries. E. Brown said she had struck him first, hitting him two or three times on the face and chest with her fist, and he struck her while trying to defend himself. He said, "Yeah, I called her a bitch because she is a bitch and always complains about my drinking. If she wouldn't bug me all the time, I wouldn't have to keep her in line." He admitted to drinking "about" five beers earlier today but at the time of our interview showed no signs of intoxication. I did not see any signs of redness or injury on E. Brown's face. He refused medical aid.

Before we left the scene I gave the victim a copy of Form #4587, entitled "Notification to Victims of Domestic Violence," which listed shelter and counseling information, right to arrest, and the report number of the incident.

I placed E. Brown under arrest for violation of CPC 273.5, Spousal Abuse, and transported him to the jail for booking. The suspect was held for $50,000 bail.

I reviewed our police department records for prior reports regarding domestic violence involving these parties. I located two other reports: DR#04-8970 dated 10-23-04 and DR#05-9983 dated 11-21-05. Copies of those reports are attached.

Case closed by arrest.

Narrative #5 - Assault and battery

INJURIES   *Victim had ½" cut on lip (photo attached)*

                                              Tag # 109834

On 1-11-11, I was on patrol in a marked police car in the area of 6000 Lime St. At approximately 1500 hours I saw a group of at least five people blocking the street. I stopped to investigate and saw that Victim Doyle and Suspect Toth were fighting on the ground. I pulled them apart and requested a follow-up officer.

I saw that Doyle was bleeding from the lip. He refused medical care and told me the fight started when Toth got upset with him when his baseball went into Toth's backyard. Doyle said he was in his own backyard playing ball with his dog, Fido. He had thrown the ball too high and the ball flew into the suspect's backyard. Doyle went to Toth's home and asked him if he could retrieve the ball. Toth became verbally abusive calling him an "ass" and started to push Doyle off the property. Doyle told Toth to stop pushing him and with that Toth punched the victim in the face with his fist. The two began fighting and ended up in the street with several neighbors standing by watching. Doyle said he never hit the suspect or called him any names.

Doyle said he and the suspect have known each other for about six years and have never liked each other. The two have been involved in two or three arguments over the years but the arguments never escalated into a fight. Doyle said he was not seriously injured. He refused medical aid. He did want the suspect arrested for assault and battery. Doyle said he would support prosecution. I took a Polaroid photo of the victim's injury and that photo is attached to this report.

Once Officer Start, #3489, arrived I had him stand by while I interviewed the suspect. After the suspect read and signed the attached Miranda advisement waiver form, he told me that he had known the victim for about five years. The victim and he have never gotten along because of an old girlfriend, Margie Parsons, whom they both liked and both had dated. The incident that started today began when the victim came to the suspect's home wanting to get a baseball in the suspect's backyard. The suspect insisted that the name-calling began when the victim called him an "ass" and "white trash" and punched him. The suspect stated that he only defended himself by striking back, hitting the victim in the face.

Witness #1, Mayer, walked up to me and told me that she had seen the fight. She said she had been in her driveway, which is next door to the suspect's home. She heard some yelling coming from the suspect's home and heard the suspect call the victim an "ass." She saw the suspect push the second victim, possibly three times before the victim even began to defend himself. She said the victim repeatedly told the suspect to stop pushing him but the suspect continued to push and shove the victim. She saw the suspect use his right fist to punch the victim in the face, which knocked the victim to the ground. She added that, as a neighbor, she knows both parties. She said she would be willing to testify.

I asked three or four additional witnesses what they saw but only Witness #2, Boyer, would talk to me. Boyer said he was talking to Mayer in her driveway when he heard Doyle and Toth arguing. He looked in the direction of the suspect's home and heard the suspect call the victim an "ass." He saw the suspect push the victim at least once and then the suspect punched the victim in the face, knocking him to the ground. He never saw the victim attempt to hit the suspect but he did hear the victim tell the suspect to "leave me alone." Mayer pointed at the suspect and said that he was the aggressor. Mayer then pointed to the victim and said that he was the victim. Mayer said that he would be willing to testify.

At 1445 hours I had the victim place the suspect under private person's arrest and accepted the suspect into my custody for booking at the jail. I transported the suspect to the jail at 1455 hours and I booked him for violation of CPC 240-242, Assault and Battery. Booking was completed at 1645 hours and the suspect was released on a citation, #459870.

Case closed by arrest.

Narrative #6 - Assault with a deadly weapon

INJURY

1 - cut on victim's forehead, between 1 inch and 1 ½ inches long (Photo of injury) Tag # 12577

EVIDENCE

1 - Baseball bat, brown wood, blood stains on upper half

1 - Men's T-shirt, size extra large, blood-stained (victim's)   Tag # 12579

On 1-11-11, at 2335 hours I was dispatched to 123 Main St. regarding a fight in the parking lot of Denny's restaurant. Officer S. Smalley, #24578, was assigned as my follow-up officer. I arrived at about 2345 hours and Officer Smalley arrived at about 2346 hours.

When I arrived, I saw the victim, Noe, sitting on the pavement in front of the restaurant, holding his head in his hands. I saw blood coming from his head and it appeared to me that he had a 1" to 1 ½" cut on his forehead. I requested the paramedics and provided a bandage for the victim. When I asked him what had happened, he pointed north, towards the suspect's vehicle, a black Ford Mustang, California License I LIK IT. The vehicle was about 25 feet away from where I was standing and where the victim was sitting. The victim said the person seated behind the wheel was the person who had hit him with a bat. I could see the suspect, Manley, seated behind the wheel of the vehicle.

I had Officer Smalley drive to the rear of the suspect's car and use the police car to block the car from leaving. Officer Smalley and I had our weapons drawn and I told the suspect to get out of the vehicle. Manley got out of the vehicle and while doing so said, "The jerk has been seeing my ex-wife and he's been asking for it—I should've killed him." I handcuffed the suspect and placed him in the back of my patrol car. I looked in the back seat of the suspect's vehicle and I saw a baseball bat. The bat had a red substance, possibly blood, on it. Officer Smalley and I searched the suspect's car but found no other weapons or contraband. I took the baseball bat out of the car to book as evidence.

The paramedics arrived at 2348 hours and attended to the victim. Paramedic Smith, #2456, stated that the victim probably had a concussion and would be transported to InterCity Hospital, 2356 Garfield, Alhambra. I took the victim's T-shirt as evidence because of the bloodstains on it. Before the victim was transported to the hospital, I took a Polaroid photo of his injury.

Officer Smalley checked the restaurant and surrounding areas for witnesses but was able to locate only one witness, Nelson. Nelson said that she had been driving northbound on Light St. when she saw Manley and Noe in the parking lot of the restaurant. She heard them yelling at each other but couldn't hear what they were saying. She saw the suspect hit the victim once on the head, with a baseball bat, and saw the victim fall down. She parked across the street and called the police on her cellular phone and waited until the police arrived. She pointed to Manley and said he was the person she had seen hit the victim. She said she would testify.

After I advised the suspect of his rights per Miranda, he signed the waiver, Form #5298, Advisement of Rights Waiver (attached). He said he knew that the victim had been dating his ex-wife and he didn't like the fact that she was dating anyone so soon after their divorce. The suspect said he followed the victim's car when the victim left the ex-wife's house this evening, at about 2300 hours. The victim drove to the restaurant and went inside for about ½ hour. The suspect waited for the victim outside and when the victim opened his car door, the suspect walked up to him, yelled "son of a bitch" at him, and then hit him once with the bat. The suspect appeared angry while he was telling me the story, because he was red faced and yelling. He added, "If you give me the chance, I'll kill him—my wife is too good for him."

Officer Smalley drove the suspect to the jail for booking for violation of CPC 245 (a) (2), Assault with a Deadly Weapon. The suspect was held on $35,000 bail. I booked the bat, shirt and photo into evidence. The suspect's vehicle was left locked in the parking lot of the restaurant. The vehicle is registered to the suspect.

159

At 0055 hours on January 3, 2011, I went to the hospital to check on the victim's condition. He was conscious and said he would remain in the hospital overnight. He had received a concussion and required six stitches in his forehead. He said that he would see to it that a copy of his medical report was forwarded to the police department to be included in this report.

He told me that he didn't know the suspect had followed him to the restaurant. He knew from talking to the suspect's ex-wife, Mary Ann Manley, that the suspect could be very jealous. He had been dating the ex-wife for two to three months and this incident was the first time he had any problem with the suspect. When he walked out of the restaurant the suspect yelled his name and then hit him on the head with the bat. The victim said he would support prosecution.

Case closed by arrest.

Narrative #7 - Drunk in public arrest

On 1-11-11, at 0120 hours Officer Smith and I were dispatched to The Sports Bar at 1234 E. Levy Street, regarding a disturbance. We arrived at 0132 hours, entered the bar and spoke to Bill Night, who said he had called the police. Night pointed to the suspect, Williams. Night said that Williams had come into the bar about one hour earlier, already intoxicated. Williams had asked Night to serve him liquor and Night refused. Night told Williams to leave because he was disturbing other customers by being loud and obnoxious. Night had seen Williams approach two or three bar customers and ask them to buy him a drink, and when they refused, Williams yelled at them and called them names like "asshole" and "butthead." Night said that he wanted Williams removed from the property for the remainder of the evening.

Officer Smith and I escorted Williams outside. I spoke to Williams and when he replied he slurred his words. Williams admitted to drinking a "few beers" earlier this date. I smelled a strong odor of an unknown type of alcohol on his breath. His clothing was in disarray and dirty. His face was red and flushed and his eyes were bloodshot. He could not stand without some assistance.

I arrested Williams for drunk in public, violation of California Penal Code Section 647(f). I drove him to the jail, where he was held for a four-hour detainment and then released.

Case closed by arrest.

Narrative #8 – Sexual Assault

EVIDENCE

1 - Pink ladies blouse, size 34   Tag # 29057

1 - Pair ladies Levis, size medium   Tag # 29058

1 - Victim rape kit   Tag # 29059

6 - Photos of victim   Tag # 29060

On 1-11-11, at 2230 hours I was dispatched to a pay phone located at 112 S. Mertle Street, Milepost Park, regarding a 911 call received from the public telephone at that location.   Dispatcher D. Lytle told me that the call had been made by an unidentified female who was crying and said she had been raped. The caller had then hung up the phone.

I arrived at about 2245 hours and found the victim , Pauley, seated next to the pay phone, crying.   When I asked her if she had called 911, she said she had done so.   Her left cheek was red and bruised and her blouse was dirty and torn.   She said she had been raped by two armed male Hispanics who then dropped her off at the park.   She provided the descriptions of the two suspects and their vehicle.   The descriptions appear on page one of this report.   At 2253 hours, a general broadcast (GB#4568709) was made to all Orange County law enforcement agencies regarding the suspects' description and their vehicle.

The victim told me the following: she had been shopping alone at the Town City Mall, 1209 Munley Street, Alhambra, until approximately 2030 hours.   She was walking back to her car, which was parked in the southeast parking lot, when she was approached by the two suspects.   Suspect #1, the driver, drove his vehicle next to her and showed her a gun and told her, "Get in the car or you're dead."   She got into the back seat with suspect #2.   Suspect #2 also had a gun and pointed it at her while suspect #1 drove to an unknown location. She was forced to lie down on the floorboard and could not see where the suspect drove.   She could not provide further information about the guns that both suspects had other than to say both guns were chrome.

She said they drove around for about ten minutes and then suspect #1 stopped the car.   Both suspects pulled her from the car.   She saw they were on an unlit dirt road in an area that she didn't recognize.   While suspect #1 pointed the gun at her, suspect #2 began to tear her clothing off. Suspect #2 kept telling her "Just do as we say and you won't get hurt." She was crying and screaming. Suspect #2 hit her on her left cheek with his fist, knocking her to the ground. She believed that she lost consciousness for a few minutes because when she woke up suspect #2 was lying on top of her, raping her. The suspect had inserted his penis into her vagina and ejaculated. Suspect #1 was still holding the gun and kept it pointed at her while suspect #2 raped her.

Both suspects then left the area in their vehicle, leaving her stranded. She managed to find her blouse and pants but could not find her panties, bra or shoes. She found her purse next to her clothing. All items were still in her purse. After finding her clothing and getting dressed, she walked for about 15 minutes until she came to the telephone in the park. She said that she would probably be able to recognize the suspects if she saw them again and would testify.

I told the victim that it would be helpful to our investigation if she would consent to a rape examination and explained to her what the examination involved. She said she would do so and I drove her to Intercommunity Hospital, 12034 Denton Ave. We arrived at the hospital at about 2355 hours. Before the victim underwent the examination, I took six Polaroid photographs of her. Dr. Marsha Gordon treated the victim. Dr. Gordon completed the rape kit and sealed it at 0100 hours. I took custody of the rape kit and later booked it into the evidence refrigerator. A copy of the doctor's report is attached to this report.

The victim called her sister from the hospital. The sister, Miriam Renton, brought additional clothing to the hospital for the victim. I took custody of the blouse and pants the victim had been wearing at the time of the assault and booked them and the photographs into evidence.

The victim consented to accompanying her sister and me to the general vicinity of the park in an attempt to locate the area where the rape had occurred. We drove in my marked police car to an unnamed dirt road that is ¼ mile east of the park, but the victim was unable to say with any certainty that this was the area where the attack occurred. I was unable to locate any of the victim's missing clothing or any signs that the attack had occurred in this area.

The victim stated she wanted to get her car from the shopping center parking lot, so at 0145 hours I drove her and her sister back to the shopping center and found her car. I checked the area around her car, a 1995 Honda Prelude, California license B BODY, for evidence and found none.

Case open; refer to investigation.

Narrative #9 - Suicide

EVIDENCE

1 - Suicide note   Tag # 129799

1 - Last Will and Testament   Tag # 129800

On 1-11-11, at 1120 hours Officer J. Smally, #3457, and I were dispatched to 2380 S. Oakleaf regarding a dead body. Dispatcher C. Quinton stated she had also dispatched the paramedics. We arrived at 1135 hours. We were met at the curb by J. Nome, who pointed to the house at 22390 S. Oakleaf Drive, next door to her own residence. She said while she was in her house, she heard one gunshot, which sounded like it had come from her neighbor's house, the one at 22390 S. Oakleaf Drive. She went next door, to 22390, saw that the garage door was up, and found her neighbor seated in a chair in the garage. She said she thought her neighbor was dead because he wasn't moving at all, there was blood on his head, and he didn't seem to be breathing. She touched nothing. She immediately called the police.

Officer Smally and I went to the front of the attached garage of the residence at 22390 S. Oakleaf Drive. The garage door was up. We saw a white male subject seated upright in a chair in the center of the garage. Nome identified the person in the chair as her neighbor, John L. Langley. I checked the man's neck for a pulse and checked for breathing, but detected neither. I looked at both eyes and saw that the pupils were dilated. It appeared that he had a wound in his left temple because there was blood coming from that area. A handgun was in the victim's left hand and there were blood splatters on the victim's left hand and on the gun. The left hand and gun rested in his lap. Officer Smally and I checked the rest of the house for additional people and found none. The house appeared neat and tidy. There was one car, a 1989 Cadillac Seville, California license RUGGED, parked in the driveway. It was locked and appeared untouched.

The paramedics arrived at 1137 hours. Paramedic J. Neery, #289, pronounced the victim dead at 1138 hours. I requested a deputy coroner and a crime scene investigator at 1140 hours.

Nome said that the victim lived alone and had been depressed for quite some time due to ill health. She said that the victim suffered from bone cancer and had been in pain for a number of months. She had last spoken to the victim at about 0730 hours this date when she saw him picking up his newspaper in his driveway. She said "hello" to him. He asked her if she would watch his dog, Mopsie, because he might be gone for a few weeks or longer. She said she would look after the dog as she often did when he would leave. She did not know if the victim had any family or relatives who lived locally. The dog was in the backyard. Nome said she would care for the dog until other arrangements could be made.

When I walked into the kitchen, I saw two pieces of paper on the kitchen table. One of the pieces of paper, approximately 3" x 5", was a hand-printed note, with the victim's name written at the bottom, as a signature would be. The note read "I can't take the pain and loneliness anymore. Please see to it that Mopsie is cared for by my neighbor." I collected the original note as evidence. The other piece of paper was approximately 8½" x 11" sheet, typewritten, with the words "Last Will and Testament of John J. Langley" typed at the top of the page. The note said that Langley was leaving all his possessions to his sister, Mary Jones, 11445 Mountain Road, South Fork, Idaho 89214, telephone (601)555-0120. There were four typewritten paragraphs, and a handwritten date and the noticeable signature of the victim at the bottom of the page. I collected the apparent will as evidence. On the kitchen counter was an opened box of ammunition; there were six bullets missing from the box, which had contained 50 bullets.

Crime scene investigator L. Golton, #289, arrived at 1148 hours and took photographs of the scene. Refer to his supplemental report.

In the kitchen, on the counter, I found two prescription bottles of medication, 1 bottle each of Prozac and Demerol, in the victim's name. By calling the pharmacy phone number listed on the label of the bottles, I was able to obtain the name of the treating physician (Dr. John Adler). I called Dr. Adler, 12098 Downey Ave., Downey, 213-555-0101, who confirmed that the victim was suffering from bone cancer. Dr. Adler said he had last seen the victim on the 19th of this month. Dr. Adler also confirmed that the victim had been in extreme pain and was extremely depressed the last time he saw him.

Coroner's Investigator W. Bueller, #12098, arrived at 1235 hours. I told him what I had learned from Nome and the doctor, and confirmed that nothing had been touched or moved. Investigator Bueller examined the scene with me and confirmed that the death appeared to be a suicide. He examined the handgun found in the victim's left hand. It was a .38 caliber revolver, Smith and Wesson Model 15, serial #292876K. He said that one bullet had been fired from the gun. An inventory of the victim's property was conducted in my presence. Items retained by Investigator Bueller were (1) the victim's wallet containing $35.00 cash, the victim's driver's license, two credit cards, and miscellaneous photographs; (2) a Timex watch; (3) a white metal ring; and (4) both bottles of prescription medication. The gun and all other items were kept by the coroner's investigator. I received an inventory of those items retained by Coroner's Investigator Bueller. That inventory is attached to this report.

I showed Bueller the will and the suicide note, and provided a copy of both for his report when I got back to the station. A coroner's van arrived at 1425 hours and the body was removed at 1435 hours. Investigator Bueller said that an autopsy would be performed the following day and I could get the final written results in two weeks.

I requested that dispatch check the registration of the vehicle in the driveway and of the handgun. According to Department of Motor Vehicles records, the vehicle was registered to the victim, and Department of Justice firearms records showed the handgun as being registered to the victim.

Case open, pending results of the autopsy.

Narrative #10 - Suicide

EVIDENCE

1 - Suicide note   Tag # 28057

On 1-11-11, at 1440 hours I was dispatched to 123 Main St. regarding an attempted suicide. Dispatcher P. Rollins told me that the female apparently attempting suicide had called on the 911 line and was crying. When Rollins asked what the problem was, the female said that she "wanted to die" and had taken "some pills." The telephone connection was then broken. Rollins said that she had obtained the address where the call had originated through the 911 operator. Rollins continued to call the phone number while I was en route to the noted address, but she got the busy tone every time she called.

The backup officer assigned to assist on this call was Officer Wefton, #498, and we both arrived at the same time, approximately 1457 hours. We went to the front door of the residence and knocked several times, each time calling out "Police." We tried to open the front door but it was locked. We did not get any response to our knocks and yells, so we walked to the rear door of the residence and found it unlocked. We entered and called out several more times "Police." I heard some moaning and, following the sound, I found the victim, Sally Ann Porter, on the floor of the front bathroom. She was semi- conscious but was unable to answer my questions about what had happened to her. I saw 4 medicine bottles on the floor and there were pills, possibly from the bottles, strewn about on the floor. Because I believed that she might have ingested some of the contents of those bottles, I requested the paramedics. I made the request at approximately 1500 hours.   I saw no injuries to her body, and it appeared that she had vomited an unknown substance onto her blouse.

While I stayed with Porter, Officer Wefton searched the remainder of the house to see if anyone else was there.   He didn't find anyone.   During his search of the house, he found a note on the kitchen table. He believed it had been written by Porter because it had her name as the signature.   The note said that she wanted to die and that she had no reason to live anymore.   A copy of the note is attached to this report.   I booked the note into evidence under Tag #28057.

The paramedics arrived at approximately 1505 hours and began to treat victim Porter. The paramedics took the medicine bottles, labeled as Valium, Codeine, Aspirin, and Paxil, to the hospital.   Porter was transported to Anaheim Memorial Hospital for further treatment.

We arrived at Anaheim Memorial Hospital at approximately 1535 hours, and a few minutes later I spoke to the attending physician, Dr. M. Yaden.   He told me that Porter had ingested an unknown amount of prescription medications, pills believed to be Valium and Codeine, from the bottles that I had found in the front bathroom. He believed that Porter had tried to commit suicide.   He said he had talked to Dr. W. Carter, the psychiatrist who had been treating Porter and who had prescribed the Valium for her.   Dr. Carter had not prescribed the Codeine for Porter.   Dr. Yaden gave me Dr. Carter's phone number and address: (714) 555-0989, 1290 West 5th St., Anaheim. The prescription bottle containing Codeine bore the name of Dr. V. Opty as the prescriber.   I couldn't talk with Dr. Opty because she was out of town.   Dr. Opty's phone number and address are: (714) 555-9909, 239 Midvale Ave., Anaheim.

I told Dr. Yaden about the 911 telephone call that Porter made and showed him the apparent suicide note.

Drs. Yaden and Carter agreed that Porter should be housed in the hospital psychiatric ward as a Danger to Self, pursuant to Welfare and Institutions Code 5150.

At 1559 hours, Porter was left in the care and custody of Dr. Yaden.

Narrative #11 - Private Person's Arrest

PROPERTY LOSS

1- Set of six wrenches, in a single package, Sears Craftsman brand, recovered; photo attached $79.00

EVIDENCE

1- Videotape of the theft   Tag # 20001

On 1-11-11, at 1915 hours Officer J. Smith, #212 and I were dispatched to 123 Main St. regarding a shoplifter in custody. I arrived at about 1930 hours. When I arrived, I spoke with witness Jones, who is the Security Manager for the store. He said that the suspect, Morales, and the other witness, Banlon, were in the Security Manager's office. He told me the following: he had been working in his office in the store at about 1856 hours this date and saw the suspect, Morales, on the closed-circuit TV which is kept in his office. He saw Morales was in the automotive department and that Morales kept looking around as if to see if anyone was looking at him. Jones radioed to his assistant, witness Banlon, and told him to watch Morales.

While Banlon made his way to the automotive department, Jones continued to watch Morales on the closed-circuit TV. Jones turned on the time-lapse video recorder and recorded the actions of Morales. Jones watched the suspect walk around the automotive tool section, take a set of wrenches off a shelf in the tool section as he walked past the shelf, and stuff the set of wrenches down the front of his pants, near the crotch area. The suspect frequently looked around as if to see whether anyone was watching him. The suspect then slowly made his way to the front of the store, walking past three open and staffed cash register stations. The suspect made no attempt to pay for the item he had stuffed in his pants. The suspect continued to walk, going out the north front doors, with Banlon approximately 6 feet behind him.

Once the suspect and Banlon were outside the store and on the sidewalk, Banlon tapped the suspect on his shoulder and asked him to return to the store. The suspect cooperated and walked back into the store with Banlon, to the Security Manager's office. Once the suspect was inside the office, Jones asked him if he knew why he had been stopped. The suspect replied "O.K., you got me - here it is", removed the package of wrenches from inside the front of his pants, and handed the package of wrenches to Banlon.

Jones told me that he wanted the suspect arrested for petty theft and would support prosecution of the suspect for that crime. Jones then took me to the Security Manager's Office, where witness Banlon was detaining the suspect. The suspect remained in the Security Manager's office with Jones and Officer Smith while I then interviewed witness Banlon. Banlon said that his manager, Jones, had told him to watch the suspect, and he did so. Banlon said he discreetly followed the suspect around in the automotive section for about five minutes and then saw the suspect pick up a set of wrenches and place it in his pants.

Banlon followed the suspect out through the store's front doors, and the suspect did not stop to pay for the wrenches. The suspect made no statements until he was brought to the office and Jones confronted him.

Banlon heard the suspect say, "O.K., you got me—here it is" and saw the suspect remove the wrenches from his pants.

Both witnesses said that they had never seen the suspect in the store before. Both witnesses identified the wrenches as belonging to their store, and pointed out the store inventory/price tag still in place on the package.

I took a Polaroid photo of the package of wrenches and returned the wrenches to Jones. The photo of the property is attached to this report. I watched the videotape of the theft and the tape clearly showed the suspect place an item down the front of his pants, then turn and leave the store without paying for that item. I took the tape as evidence and booked it under Evidence Tag #20001.

I provided the suspect with Form 238, Advisement of Rights. I read and explained those rights to him, and he signed the form, signifying that he understood his rights. He refused to talk with me about the charges against him. I searched the suspect and found $3.00 in U.S. currency. I found no other means by which the suspect could have paid for the item he had taken.

Jones told the suspect that he was under arrest for theft, violation of California Penal Code section 484/488. I transported the suspect to the jail for booking. The suspect was later released on Citation No. DE239479. Case closed by arrest.

Narrative #12 - Warrant arrest

On 1-11-11, at approximately 1500 hours I was on patrol in a marked police car, driving westbound in the 6000 block of Lincoln Avenue, when I saw the suspect, Smith, driving a blue 1969 Chevrolet El Camino, California license 230TTT, ahead of me and also westbound on Lincoln, approaching the intersection of Lincoln and Valley View. Smith failed to stop his vehicle at the stop sign at the corner of westbound Lincoln and northbound Valley View before he turned northbound onto Valley View. The failure to stop was a violation of California Vehicle Code section 22450. I was directly behind Smith when I saw the violation. I stopped my car at that stop sign and then turned right onto northbound Valley View. I was again directly behind Smith.

I turned on my patrol car's overhead lights and siren and Smith immediately pulled his vehicle to the east curb of northbound Valley View. When I walked up to his vehicle, I saw that he was alone. He was perspiring heavily on the forehead, even though the driver's side window was down and the outside temperature was about 60 degrees (Fahrenheit). I asked him if something was wrong and he said, "No." I told him why I had stopped him (failure to stop at the stop sign) and I asked to see his driver's license. He said that he had forgotten to bring his license with him. He said the vehicle was registered to him. I asked him to get out of his vehicle, and he did. He told me his name and date of birth and I radioed that information to dispatch. Dispatch told me that there was a warrant for Smith's arrest for burglary, California Penal Code section 459.

Officer R. Smolten, #3736, who was assigned as my follow-up officer, arrived approximately two minutes later. I then told Smith he was under arrest pursuant to the warrant, and I handcuffed him. He offered no resistance, and said, "I knew my luck couldn't last forever." I searched him and found nothing except a wallet containing $5.00 cash. Smith asked that I let his wife pick up the vehicle instead of having it towed. I told him he could call his wife from the police station to arrange to have the vehicle picked up.

I cited Smith for the stop sign violation, Citation #493766. I drove Smith to the Cypress City Jail for booking on the warrant. Case closed by arrest.

Warrant #384590098. Issued 4-7-95 by Judge D. Bice, Orange County Superior Court (West), charging violation of California Penal Code section 459, Burglary. Bail $25,000.00

Narrative #13 - Possession of a controlled substance

EVIDENCE

1 - 2" x 2" clear cellophane baggie containing white powder, 1.2 grams   Tag # 38456

2 - 2" x 2" empty, clear cellophane baggie with white residue   Tag # 38457

On 1-11-11, at approximately 0700 hours Officer Verry, #456, and I were on patrol in a marked police car in the 2100 block of State College Blvd., when I saw the suspect, Reynolds, driving a 1979 red Chevrolet Corvette, California license 202HJH. I saw the car make a U-turn in front of the driveway to the fire station at 2150 State College Boulevard. That U-turn was a violation of California Vehicle Code (CVC) Section 22104.

I turned on my patrol car's overhead lights and siren and Reynolds stopped his car at the north curb line of State College Blvd. When I walked up to Reynolds as he sat in his car, I saw that he was alone. He appeared to be quite nervous because when I asked for his driver's license he fumbled for his wallet and started to sweat profusely on his hands and forehead. As he opened up his wallet a cellophane baggie, containing a white powder, fell out onto the pavement. I looked at the baggie and then looked at Reynolds. He said, "I don't know how that got there, officer—it isn't mine." I said to him, "It was in your wallet." Reynolds said, "I don't know if I want to talk to you now." I looked at Reynolds' nose and saw white dust particles at the opening of his nostrils. I looked into his nostrils and saw white dust particles clinging to his nose hairs. Based upon my training and experience, the substance in the baggie looked like cocaine, and I know that cocaine is commonly sniffed or "snorted" into the nose. I had Reynolds get out of the car, handcuffed him and told him that he was under arrest for Possession of a Controlled Substance, a violation of California Health and Safety (H&S) Code Section 11350.

While Officer Verry watched Reynolds, I searched the interior of Reynolds' car. I found two more baggies under the driver's seat. They were of the same type that Reynolds had dropped. Both bags were empty, but had a white residue on the inside.

Reynolds' car was towed for storage pursuant to CVC 22651 (h)(1). The registration showed that it was registered to him.

Officer Verry and I drove Reynolds to the station for booking. When we arrived, I immediately Valtox-tested the contents of the first baggie. It tested positive for cocaine. During booking, I examined Reynolds for signs of being under the influence of cocaine. He displayed no such symptoms.

I read Reynolds' Miranda rights to him from Form 238. After I read and explained those rights to him, Reynolds signed the attached form, agreeing to waive his rights and said, "Sure, I'll talk to you." He said that the drug was cocaine and he had purchased the drug the day before from a man he knows only by the name of "Jolly." He did not know where "Jolly" lived but he could always find him at a local bar called "Samy's," located at Thorpe and Walnut Street, in Orange.

Reynolds described "Jolly" as a male white, 30-35 years, 5-9", 175 lbs, black hair. He said he paid $20 for the bag. The empty bags that I found under the seat were old. Reynolds said that he had taken the drug the night before, at about 6:00 p.m. He said he uses cocaine about three to four times a week and has been doing so for about three months.

Reynolds was booked for violation of CVC section 22104 and California H&S Code section 11350 and was held for $25,000.00 bail. Case closed by arrest.

SAMPLES OF ACTUAL POLICE REPORT FORMS

The next section is a collection of police reports from various agencies. The intent is for you to become familiar with them and quite possibly comfortable enough to be immediately confident in your ability to complete an investigation. Read each form several times and if you want to take it to the next level, make copies of each form and practice filling in the blanks.

Miranda Advisement Form(Page 174): Read to a suspect; each question is acknowledged by a signature prior to being questioned as part of a criminal investigation.

Impound Form(Page 175): Used whenever a vehicle is impounded or stored by an officer. It includes vehicle identification information and an inventory of the vehicles contents.

Alarm Activation Report(Page 176): Completed when an officer responds to an alarm activation at a business or home. It documents response and status of the location.

Crime Scene Investigation(Pages 177-178): Completed by the Crime Scene Investigator; documents evidence observed or collected at the scene.

Crime Summary Report(Pages 179-180): Written after the investigating officer concludes that a crime has occurred. It must include all of the elements of the crime and should include all information regarding the crime at the time the report was taken, such as location, the time and place the crime occurred, loss or injuries, evidence collected, suspect description, etc. It can be used to document any criminal occurrence.

Domestic Violence Report(Pages 181-182): Used during a domestic violence investigation documenting the current incident and prior history of the suspects and victims.

Field Interview Card(Pages 183-184): Used to document field contacts in various locations to be used in future investigations such as Probation, Parole, and criminal offenses.

Traffic Collision Report(Pages 185-186): Provides information regarding traffic collisions. Such reports typically include statements of drivers and witnesses, diagrams, and photographs.

Supplemental Report(Pages 187-188): Typically written by an officer other than the original reporting officer. For instance, an officer may assist a fellow officer in an investigation by interviewing people or by recovering property. The assisting officer would write a Supplemental Report to document his or her actions.

Citizens Arrest Form(Page 189): Completed when a misdemeanor occurs which is not observed by the officer, but by a private citizen. It documents the desire for prosecution of the arrestee.

Traffic Violation(Page 190): Issued when a traffic or parking violation has occurred.

Parking Ticket(Page 191): Issued for Municipal or County parking violations that are paid directly to the issuing agency.

Suspected Child Abuse Report(Page 192): Used to initiate a child abuse investigation documenting all involved parties or those with knowledge of the situation. This form is used by mandated child abuse reporters.

Booking Slip(Pages 193-194): Completed when booking a suspect into any detention facility for confirmation of the arrestee's identity and documentation of the basic elements of the crime.

Driving Under the Influence Investigation Report(Page 195): A narcotic, drunk driving, or intoxication report is used to describe the suspect's condition of being under the influence of a drug or alcohol. Most often, these are separate reports and written in conjunction with a crime report.

DUI Field Interview(Page 196): This documents the field interview and field sobriety testing performed by the arresting officer.

Short Form Shoplifting Report(Pages 197-198): Used to record observation and arrest information provided by the arresting private party such as security and loss prevention officers.

Identity Theft Report(Pages 199-200): Used by Investigators or officers to record identity theft information usually provided by the victim of the crime. Listed in the report are all account numbers that have been compromised.

STATEMENT FORM ADVISEMENT OF RIGHTS

Date: _____   CI #

1. **You have the right to remain silent.**

   Do you understand? _____

2. **Anything you say may be used against you in court.**

   Do you understand? _____

3. **You have the right to an attorney before and during any questioning.**

   Do you understand? _____

4. **If you cannot afford an attorney, one will be appointed for you before questioning, if you wish.**

   Do you understand? _____

Expressed Waiver: Can we talk about what happened? _____

                                   Signature _____

Advising Officer: _____

Witness: _____

Date: _____

☐ IMPOUND	☐ 30 DAY IMPOUND	☐ STORED (VEHICLE REPORT)	☐ RECOVERY	☐ OUTSIDE AGENCY RECOVERY

REPORTING DEPARTMENT	LOCATION CODE	DATE/TIME REPORTED	CITATION NUMBER	CASE NUMBER

LOCATION TAKEN / RECOVERED FROM	STORAGE AUTHORITY	DISTRICT	GRID

TOWING COMPANY / PERSON TAKING POSSESSION OF VEHICLES	HOLD REQUEST FOR (REQUIRED ON ALL IMPOUNDS)	VIN CONDITION	YES	NO
	☐ TRAFFIC ☐ 30 DAY HOLD 14602.6 ☐ CRIME SCENE INVESTIGATIONS ☐ INVESTIGATIONS ☐ OUTSIDE AGENCY REQUEST	VIN APPEARS ALTERED VIN COMPARES TO REGISTRATION	☐ ☐	☐ ☐

RECOVERED VEHICLE INFORMATION / CLETS ENTRY

FCN	ORIGINAL CASE NUMBER	STATUS	RECOVERY DATE	REPORTING AGENCY

NAME OF PERSON OR AGENCY NOTIFIED	DATE/TIME NOTIFIED	HOW NOTIFIED	RETURNED TO OWNER
		☐ PHONE ☐ IN PERSON ☐ BY MAIL ☐ TELETYPE	☐ YES ☐ NO

VEHICLE DESCRIPTION / OWNERSHIP

LICENSE PLATE	☐ FRONT ☐ NONE ☐ BACK	Month/Year	State	Year	Make	Model	Body Type	Color (combination)

VIN										Engine Number (Required for

Registered Owner	Address	Zip Code	Telephone(s) (Home / Business / Cell)

Legal Owner	Address	Zip Code	Telephone(s) (Home / Business / Cell)

VEHICLE CONDITION AND INVENTORY
(USE REMARKS SPACE AT BOTTOM FOR NEEDED DETAILS)

Odometer Reading	Digital ☐	Driveable ☐ YES ☐ NO ☐ UNKNOWN		CSI BY	ID #	Latent Prints Taken ☐ YES ☐ NO ☐ PENDING	PHOTOGRAPHED ☐ YES ☐ NO ☐ PENDING	DNA ☐ YES ☐ NO ☐ PENDING

CONDITION	YES	NO	ITEMS	YES	NO	ITEMS	YES	NO	TIRES/WHEELS	YES	NO	IGNITION	YES	NO	REMARKS
WRECKED			SEAT (FRONT)			REGISTRATION			LEFT FRONT			PUNCHED/PULLED			
BURNED			SEAT (BACK)			ALT/GENERATOR			RIGHT FRONT			BROKEN COLUMN			
VANDALIZED			RADIO/FACEPLATE			BATTERY			LEFT REAR			HOT WIRED			
ENG/TRANS STRIP			TAPE/CD			DIFFERENTIAL			RIGHT REAR			LOCKS TAMPERED			
MISC PARTS STRIP			TAPES/CD (#)			TRANSMISSION			SPARE(S)			WINDOWS BROKEN			
BODY METAL STRIP			TELEVISION			AUTOMATIC ( )			HUB CAPS (#)			SHAVED KEY			
			CAMPER			MANUAL ( )						VEHICLE VALUE	$		

NARRATIVE
D-Driver A-Arrestee S-Suspect W-Witness C-Contacted R-Reporting Person P-Parent M-Mentioned

Code	Name	(REQUIRED FOR ALL CVC 14601 /12500/14602.6 IMPOUNDS)	D.O.B.	Related Case number(s)	IN CUSTODY ☐ YES ☐ NO

Home Address	Phone	CDL

Driver Notification	Time	Tow Notification	Time	Prior 12500 / 14601 ☐ YES ☐ NO	If YES, Number of Priors _____	When (Mo/Yr) _____ / _____

DAMAGE (SHADE IN AREA)

Right side

Front

Rear

Left Side

FCN: (For Records Use Only)

☐ NARRATIVE CONTINUED

Storage Log Entered By	ID#	Date/Time	Garage Agent/Person Taking Possession Of Vehicle (Signature)	Date/Time

Report By	ID#	Date	District	Watch	Shift	Supervisor Authorizing Storage/Impound	Report Review By	ID#

Records Report Review	Distribution: Original-Records Pink-Traffic Gold-District Inv. Yellow-Tow Comp	Distribution by/date

ALARM ACTIVATION REPORT
CRIME PREVENTION, (714) 245-8716

CI:

DATE:

CRIME ☐   FALSE ☐

TIME:

211 ☐   459 ☐

NAME: RESIDENCE?
                                                   Yes or No
                                                   ☐   ☐

ADDRESS:

APT./SUITE #:

REPORTING PARTY:

CAUSE OF ALARM ACTIVATION	AREAS CHECKED
☐ EMPLOYEE	☐ ROOF
☐ CLEANING SERVICE	☐ PERIMETER
☐ ALARM CO./REPAIR	☐ YARD/STORAGE
☐ OTHER	

RESPONSIBLE PARTY

☐ NOT CONTACTED

☐ RESPONSIBLE/EMPLOYEE PRESENT UPON ARRIVAL:

NAME:_____

☐ RESPONSIBLE REFUSED TO RESPOND

REPORT BY: BADGE #:

COMMENTS:

DISTRIBUTION: WHITE: RECORDS   YELLOW: CRIME PREVENTION   GREEN: PROPERTY OWNER   P-91 Rev 7/05

CS.2

176

CRIME SCENE INVESTIGATION REPORT

CI# _____ Pg. _____ of _____

PC 459 – Res _____ Veh _____ Comm _____ CVC 10851 _____ PC 496 _____ PC 273.5 _____

PC 211 – Res _____ Veh _____ Comm _____ PC 245 – Shooting _____ Stabbing _____ Other _____

PC 187 _____ Suicide _____ PC 261 _____ PC 243 _____ PC 242 _____ PC 288 _____ Arson _____

901 – T _____ Other Offense(s) _____ _____ _____ _____ _____

Date/Time	Location	Requested by

Victim(s)/Business		P.O.E.

Arrestee(s) _____/Suspect(s) _____ DOB

_____ Smashed/Broken
_____ Punched
_____ Pried Open
_____ Other _____

Victim Vehicle _____   Suspect Vehicle _____

_____

_____

_____

Prints: Locker #2   Eliminations

P.O.E. _____ Int. _____ Ext. _____ Window Screen _____   Yes _____ No _____

Doors _____ Windows _____ Side Mirrors _____ Sliding Glass Door _____ Victim Not Present _____

Rear View Mirror _____ Car Door _____ Negative Results _____

Other _____ _____

Photos: Locker #2   Color _____ B/W _____   Standards   Type

O/A _____ Int _____ Footprints _____ None _____   Sketch _____ Vict _____ Sus _____ _____

M/R _____ Ext _____ Toolmarks _____   Factual _____ Transfers

C/U _____ P.O.E. _____ Tiremarks/Skidmarks _____   Vict _____ Sus _____ _____

Other _____ _____ _____

EVIDENCE: Locker # _____

_____

_____

_____

Reporting Officer:	I.D.#	Date of Report

A-113 (REV. 8-90) CS-177

CI# _____ Pg. _____ of _____

Summary of observations/descriptions

_____
_____
_____
_____
_____
_____
_____
_____
_____
_____
_____
_____
_____
_____
_____
_____
_____
_____
_____
_____
_____
_____
_____
_____
_____
_____
_____
_____
_____
_____
_____
_____
_____
_____
_____
_____
_____
_____
_____

Reporting Officer   ID#   Date of Report   Approved by

POLICE DEPARTMENT

TYPE REPORT

☐ Crime-Only   ☐ W&I 300-600 Involved
☐ Crime-Arrest   ☐ Domestic Violence Involved
☐ Crime-Suspect   ☐ Gang Related
☐ Information Only   ☐ CPC 293 Advisement
☐ Warrant/Parole Arrest   Release Info ? ☐ Yes ☐ No

Case #

PAGE   OF

CRIME SUMMARY

A

PRIMARY CRIME TYPE		SECONDARY CRIME TYPE	
OTHER CRIME TYPE		OTHER CRIME TYPE	

WHEN OCCURRED	DAY	DATE	TIME	TO	DAY	DATE	TIME	WHEN REPORTED	DAY	DATE	TIME

WHERE OCCURRED NUMBERS, DIRECTION, STREET, APT.#, ZIP CODE	DISTRICT	GRID #

SUSPECT VEHICLE DESCRIPTION, LIC #, STATE, YR, MK, MODEL, STYLE, COLORS	VICTIM VEHICLE (IF TARGET) LIC#, YR, MAKE, MODEL

PROPERTY ☐ LOSS ☐ NO LOSS	VALUE OF LOSS/RECOVERY $ /	CSI BY	ID #	WHERE LATENT PRINTS TAKEN? ☐ Y ☐ N

LIST PERSONS IN FOLLOWING ORDER

VB Victim Business   V Victim   W Witness   C Contacted   R Reporting Person   P Parent   M Mentioned

GROUP ALL PERSONS OF THE SAME CODE TOGETHER AND NUMBER EACH PERSON IN THE GROUP
EXAMPLE: V#1, V#2, V#3, W#1, W#2, P#1, P#2, ETC.

B

CODE	#	NAME	LAST, FIRST, MIDDLE	SEX	RACE	AGE	DOB	☐ ADULT ☐ JUV.	INTERPRETER NEEDED! ☐ TYPE–
HOME ADDRESS INCLUDE ZIP CODE				BUSINESS ADDRESS INCLUDE ZIP CODE					
HOME PHONE	HOURS	BUSINESS PHONE	HOURS	OTHER PHONE/PAGER #		CDL NUMBER / SS NUMBER			

CODE	#	NAME	LAST, FIRST, MIDDLE	SEX	RACE	AGE	DOB	☐ ADULT ☐ JUV.	INTERPRETER NEEDED! ☐ TYPE–
HOME ADDRESS INCLUDE ZIP CODE				BUSINESS ADDRESS INCLUDE ZIP CODE					
HOME PHONE	HOURS	BUSINESS PHONE	HOURS	OTHER PHONE/PAGER #		CDL NUMBER / SS NUMBER			

CODE	#	NAME	LAST, FIRST, MIDDLE	SEX	RACE	AGE	DOB	☐ ADULT ☐ JUV.	INTERPRETER NEEDED! ☐ TYPE–
HOME ADDRESS INCLUDE ZIP CODE				BUSINESS ADDRESS INCLUDE ZIP CODE					
HOME PHONE	HOURS	BUSINESS PHONE	HOURS	OTHER PHONE/PAGER #		CDL NUMBER / SS NUMBER			

C

REPORTING OFFICER	ID#	DATE	TIME	DISTRICT	WATCH
REPORT REVIEWED BY	ID#	DATE	TIME	SGT. APPROVING ARREST	

RECORDS REVIEW _____

DISTRIBUTION   TOTAL COPIES _____   DISTRIBUTION BY/DATE _____

☐ ACCIDENT BOX	☐ COURT LIAISON	☐ ORANGEWOOD	☐ TEAM POLICING	☐ OFCR _____
☐ ANIMAL CONTROL	☐ CRIMES AGAINST PERSON	☐ EVIDENCE	☐ TRAFFIC	☐ OTHER _____
☐ DISTRICT INV.	☐ CRIME PREVENTION	☐ SAPD JAIL	☐ VICE	☐ OTHER _____
☐ CII	☐ INTELLIGENCE	☐ NARCOTICS	☐ ARSON	☐ FAX # _____
☐ JUVENILE HALL	☐ STATS	☐ RAP	☐ SGT. _____	☐ GANGS _____

A Arrestee   S Suspect   JD Juvenile Detention

CODE	#	NAME	LAST, FIRST, MIDDLE	CHARGE		
RACE	SEX	☐ ADULT ☐ JUV.	AGE	DOB	HEIGHT	WEIGHT	HAIR	EYES	BUILD	BOOKING # / CITE #	BOOKING DATE

HOME ADDRESS   NUMBERS, DIRECTION, STREET, CITY, STATE, ZIP CODE   HOME PHONE

OCCUPATION & BUSINESS ADDRESS   BUSINESS PHONE

LOCATION ARRESTED   ☐ SAME AS LOCATION OF CRIME   DT ARRESTED   TIME ARRESTED

DRIVERS LIC. #/STATE   SOCIAL SECURITY #   CII #   MUG #   OCJ BOOKING #   ☐ UNDOCUMENTED PERSONI

AKA'S   TATTOOS, MARKS, SCARS, ODDITIES & LOCATIONS   CLOTHING AT TIME OF ARREST

BAIL AMOUNT   TIME RELEASED LOCATION HELD   OUTSTANDING WARRANTS/PAROLE OR PROBATION HOLDS

CODE	#	NAME	LAST, FIRST, MIDDLE	CHARGE
RACE	SEX	☐ ADULT ☐ JUV.	AGE	DOB	HEIGHT	WEIGHT	HAIR	EYES	BUILD	BOOKING # / CITE #	BOOKING DATE	BOOKING TIME

HOME ADDRESS   NUMBERS, DIRECTION, STREET, CITY, STATE, ZIP CODE   HOME PHONE

OCCUPATION & BUSINESS ADDRESS   BUSINESS PHONE

LOCATION ARRESTED   ☐ SAME AS LOCATION OF CRIME   DT ARRESTED   TIME ARRESTED

DRIVERS LIC. #/STATE   SOCIAL SECURITY #   CII #   MUG #   OCJ BOOKING #   ☐ UNDOCUMENTED PERSONI

AKA'S   TATTOOS, MARKS, SCARS, ODDITIES & LOCATIONS   CLOTHING AT TIME OF ARREST

BAIL AMOUNT   TIME RELEASED LOCATION HELD   OUTSTANDING WARRANTS/PAROLE OR PROBATION HOLDS

D

CODE	#	NAME	LAST, FIRST, MIDDLE	CHARGE
RACE	SEX	☐ ADULT ☐ JUV.	AGE	DOB	HEIGHT	WEIGHT	HAIR	EYES	BUILD	BOOKING # / CITE #	BOOKING DATE	BOOKING TIME

HOME ADDRESS   NUMBERS, DIRECTION, STREET, CITY, STATE, ZIP CODE   HOME PHONE

OCCUPATION & BUSINESS ADDRESS   BUSINESS PHONE

LOCATION ARRESTED   ☐ SAME AS LOCATION OF CRIME   DT ARRESTED   TIME ARRESTED

DRIVERS LIC. #/STATE   SOCIAL SECURITY #   CII #   MUG #   OCJ BOOKING #   ☐ UNDOCUMENTED PERSONI

AKA'S   TATTOOS, MARKS, SCARS, ODDITIES & LOCATIONS   CLOTHING AT TIME OF ARREST

BAIL AMOUNT   TIME RELEASED LOCATION HELD   OUTSTANDING WARRANTS/PAROLE OR PROBATION HOLDS

CODE	#	NAME	LAST, FIRST, MIDDLE	CHARGE
RACE	SEX	☐ ADULT ☐ JUV.	AGE	DOB	HEIGHT	WEIGHT	HAIR	EYES	BUILD	BOOKING # / CITE #	BOOKING DATE	BOOKING TIME

HOME ADDRESS   NUMBERS, DIRECTION, STREET, CITY, STATE, ZIP CODE   HOME PHONE

OCCUPATION & BUSINESS ADDRESS   BUSINESS PHONE

LOCATION ARRESTED   ☐ SAME AS LOCATION OF CRIME   DT ARRESTED   TIME ARRESTED

DRIVERS LIC. #/STATE   SOCIAL SECURITY #   CII #   MUG #   OCJ BOOKING #   ☐ UNDOCUMENTED PERSONI

AKA'S   TATTOOS, MARKS, SCARS, ODDITIES & LOCATIONS   CLOTHING AT TIME OF ARREST

BAIL AMOUNT   TIME RELEASED LOCATION HELD   OUTSTANDING WARRANTS/PAROLE OR PROBATION HOLDS

☐ MORE NAMES LISTED ON CONTINUATION SHEETS

E | FACTUAL CIRCUMSTANCES SUMMARY (NO NARRATIVE)

PER CPC 293, the victim was advised and they do/do not want the report to be public information.

DOMESTIC VIOLENCE REPORT

CI# [   ]

PAGE 1 OF _____

LOCATION OF INCIDENT		TIME OCCURRED	TIME REPORTED

CODES: V- Victim S- Suspect (primary aggressor) P - Involved Party Only

CODE	#	NAME	LAST, FIRST, MIDDLE	DOB	SEX	RACE	CDL OR ID CARD NUMBER	
		HOME ADDRSS INCLUDE ZIP CODE		PHONE NUMBER	HEIGHT	WEIGHT	HAIR	EYES
CODE	#	NAME	LAST, FIRST, MIDDLE	DOB	SEX	RACE	CDL OR ID CARD NUMBER	
		HOME ADDRSS INCLUDE ZIP CODE		PHONE NUMBER	HEIGHT	WEIGHT	HAIR	EYES

RELATIONSHIP OF INVOLVED PARTIES
(Mark all that apply)

- ☐ Married
- ☐ Divorced
- ☐ Cohabitants
- ☐ Former Co-Habitants
- ☐ Dating
- ☐ Formerly Dating
- ☐ Same Sex
- ☐ Emancipated Minor
- ☐ Engaged
- ☐ Child from Relationship # of children: _____

Duration of Relationship: Years _____ Months _____

EXISTING RESTRAINING ORDERS

Issued? ☐ YES ☐ NO
Issuing Court: _____
Order/Docket # _____

On file? ☐ YES ☐ NO
PD Case # _____
Agency: _____

- ☐ Current
- ☐ Expired
- ☐ Emergency
- ☐ Temporary
- ☐ Permanent
- ☐ Other:

CONDITION OF VICTIM

- ☐ Angry
- ☐ Apologetic
- ☐ Crying
- ☐ Fearful
- ☐ Hysterical
- ☐ Calm
- ☐ Pregnant
- ☐ Irrational
- ☐ Nervous
- ☐ Threatening
- ☐ Complaint of Pain
- ☐ Bruise
- ☐ Abrasion/Scratches
- ☐ Minor Cut
- ☐ Laceration
- ☐ Fracture
- ☐ Concussion
- ☐ Drinking/Drugs
- ☐ Strangulation
- ☐ Other/ Explain:

CONDITION OF SUSPECT

- ☐ Angry
- ☐ Apologetic
- ☐ Crying
- ☐ Fearful
- ☐ Hysterical
- ☐ Calm
- ☐ Pregnant
- ☐ Irrational
- ☐ Nervous
- ☐ Threatening
- ☐ Complaint of Pain
- ☐ Bruise
- ☐ Abrasion/Scratches
- ☐ Minor Cut
- ☐ Laceration
- ☐ Fracture
- ☐ Concussion
- ☐ Drinking/Drugs
- ☐ Strangulation
- ☐ Other/ Explain:

MEDICAL TREATMENT (VICTIM)

- ☐ None
- ☐ First Aid
- ☐ Paramedics
- ☐ Hospital
- ☐ Will see own Doctor
- ☐ Refused Medical Aid

Medic Name/ID:

Medic Name/ID:

Hospital:

Attending Physician:

MEDICAL TREATMENT (SUSPECT)

- ☐ None
- ☐ First Aid
- ☐ Paramedics
- ☐ Hospital
- ☐ Will see own Doctor
- ☐ Refused Medical Aid

Medic Name/ID:

Medic Name/ID:

Hospital:

Attending Physician:

REPORTING OFFICER	ID#	DATE	TIME	DISTRICT	WATCH

181

DOMESTIC VIOLENCE REPORT
PAGE 2 OF _____

CI# _____

HISTORY		WEAPONS INVOLVED (check all that apply)

HISTORY

Prior History of Domestic Violence? ☐ YES ☐ NO
Prior History of Violence Documented? ☐ YES ☐ NO
Number of Prior Incidents: _____
Investigating Agency: _____
Case # (s) _____

WEAPONS INVOLVED (check all that apply)

☐ Open Hand   ☐ Shoes/Boots
☐ Closed Fist   ☐ Other
☐ Firearm   List: _____
  Type: _____
☐ Knife   _____
  Type: _____
_____

WITNESSES

Witnesses present during DV? ☐ YES ☐ NO
Statements taken? ☐ YES ☐ NO
Children present during DV? ☐ YES ☐ NO
Name(s) and Age(s) of Children:

Weapon seized? ☐ YES ☐ NO   •   Evidence? ☐ YES ☐ NO
72 hour hold? ☐ YES ☐ NO   OK to release? ☐ YES ☐ NO

Party # _____ prohibited from   YES ☐ NO ☐
owning per PC 12021?   CII #:

WITNESSES / CONTACTS
(In criminal cases, you must list name and address of victim's nearest relative)

CODE	#	NAME	LAST, FIRST, MIDDLE	DOB	CDL OR ID CARD NUMBER

HOME ADDRSS INCLUDE ZIP CODE	PHONE NUMBER	SEX	RACE

CODE	#	NAME	LAST, FIRST, MIDDLE	DOB	CDL OR ID CARD NUMBER

HOME ADDRSS INCLUDE ZIP CODE	PHONE NUMBER	SEX	RACE

PHOTOGRAPHS

Photos Taken? ☐ YES ☐ NO
☐ Poloraid ☐ 35mm ☐ Other
Number taken: _____
Victim's Injuries: ☐ YES ☐ NO
Suspect's Injuries: ☐ YES ☐ NO
Weapon used: ☐ YES ☐ NO

Photographer: _____

OTHER EVIDENCE

Authorization to Release Medical Records

I authorize release of my medical records which relate to this crime report to the Santa Ana Police Department or the District Attorney's Office for the date(s) _____. The facility and/or staff providing the treatment are released from the responsibility of confidentiality as to those records which relate to diagnosis or treatment on the date(s) shown above. I may withdraw this authorization at any time before the hospital or medical providers have complied and released the information.

_____   _____   _____
PRINT NAME   SIGNATURE   DATE

NARRATIVE

_____

_____

_____

_____

_____

NARRATIVE CONTINUED ☐

NAME / LAST	FIRST	MIDDLE	AKA / MONIKER

ADDRESS	HOME PHONE

WORK ADDRESS / SCHOOL	WORK PHONE	CELL PHONE

☐ PED ☐ DRIVER ☐ BICYCLE
☐ AUTO ☐ PASS / SEAT POSITION ____

SCARS, TATOOS, ODDITIES

SEX	RACE	AGE	D.O.B.	HT.	WT.	CDL / SOC. SEC. / OTHER ID	STATE

LOCATION	DATE	TIME / MILITARY

HAIR STYLE
- SHAVEN
- BUZZED
- STRAIGHT
- COMBED BK
- WAVY
- SHORT
- SHOULDER
- LONG
- BALD
- AFRO

FACIAL HAIR
- MOUSTACHE
- GOATEE
- BEARD
- CLEAN SHVN
- UNSHAVEN
- PEACH FUZZ
- FU-MAN-CHU
- OTHER

COMPLEXION
- DARK
- LIGHT
- FAIR
- MEDIUM
- ACNE
- POC-MARKS
- SCARRED
- OTHER

BUILD
- HEAVY
- MEDIUM
- THIN
- MUSCULAR
- OTHER

HAIR COLOR

EYE COLOR

☐ GLASSES

CLOTHING / COLOR
- SHIRT _____
- DRESS _____
- JACKET _____
- SKIRT _____
- PANTS _____
- HAT _____
- SHOES _____

(RECORDS USE ONLY) / FI#

YEAR	MAKE	MODEL	STYLE	COLOR	LIC / STATE	CASE / INCIDENT #

VEHICLE ODDITIES	PROBATION / PAROLE CDC # _____
REASON FOR CONTACT	P.O. NAME CRIMINAL HISTORY

GANG AFFILIATION	GANG NAME	CITY OF GANG	
☐ YES			

ASSOCIATES / NAME / DOB	THUMB PRINT	FI CARD #
		OF

OFFICER	BADGE NUMBER	

P-25 C.S. 65 (REVISED 04-2011)

TRAFFIC COLLISION REPORT

SPECIAL CONDITIONS	NUMBER INJURED	HIT & RUN FELONY ☐	CITY		JUDICIAL DISTRICT	LOCAL REPORT NUMBER
	NUMBER KILLED	HIT & RUN MISDEMEANOR ☐	COUNTY	REPORTING DISTRICT BEAT	DAY OF WEEK S M T W T F S	TOW AWAY ☐ YES ☐ NO

LOCATION

COLLISION OCCURRED ON	MO. DAY YEAR	TIME (2400)	NCIC #	OFFICER I.D.

MILEPOST INFORMATION		GPS COORDINATES		PHOTOGRAPHS BY: ☐ NONE
FEET/MILES OF		LATITUDE LONGITUDE		
☐ AT INTERSECTION WITH			STATE HWY REL	
☐ OR: FEET/MILES OF			☐ YES ☐ NO	

PARTY 1

DRIVER'S LICENSE NUMBER	STATE	CLASS	AIR BAG	SAFETY EQUIP.	VEH. YEAR	MAKE/MODEL/COLOR	LICENSE NUMBER	STATE

DRIVER ☐ | NAME (FIRST, MIDDLE, LAST)

PEDES-TRIAN ☐ | STREET ADDRESS

OWNER'S NAME ☐ SAME AS DRIVER

PARKED VEHICLE ☐ | CITY/STATE/ZIP

OWNER'S ADDRESS ☐ SAME AS DRIVER

DISPOSITION OF VEHICLE ON ORDERS OF: ☐ OFFICER   ☐ DRIVER   ☐ OTHER

BICY-CLIST ☐ | SEX | HAIR | EYES | HEIGHT | WEIGHT | BIRTHDATE Mo. Day Year | RACE

PRIOR MECHANICAL DEFECTS: ☐ NONE APPARENT   ☐ REFER TO NARRATIVE

OTHER ☐ | HOME PHONE | BUSINESS PHONE

VEHICLE IDENTIFICATION NUMBER:

INSURANCE CARRIER   POLICY NUMBER

VEHICLE TYPE | DESCRIBE VEHICLE DAMAGE   SHADE IN DAMAGED AREA
☐ UNK.   ☐ NONE   ☐ MINOR
☐ MOD.   ☐ MAJOR   ☐ ROLL-OVER

DIR OF TRAVEL | ON STREET OR HIGHWAY | SPEED LIMIT

CA _____ DOT _____
CAL-T _____ TCP/PSC _____ MC/MX _____

PARTY 2

DRIVER'S LICENSE NUMBER	STATE	CLASS	AIR BAG	SAFETY EQUIP.	VEH. YEAR	MAKE/MODEL/COLOR	LICENSE NUMBER	STATE

DRIVER ☐ | NAME (FIRST, MIDDLE, LAST)

PEDES-TRIAN ☐ | STREET ADDRESS

OWNER'S NAME ☐ SAME AS DRIVER

PARKED VEHICLE ☐ | CITY/STATE/ZIP

OWNER'S ADDRESS ☐ SAME AS DRIVER

DISPOSITION OF VEHICLE ON ORDERS OF: ☐ OFFICER   ☐ DRIVER   ☐ OTHER

BICY-CLIST ☐ | SEX | HAIR | EYES | HEIGHT | WEIGHT | BIRTHDATE Mo. Day Year | RACE

PRIOR MECHANICAL DEFECTS: ☐ NONE APPARENT   ☐ REFER TO NARRATIVE

OTHER ☐ | HOME PHONE | BUSINESS PHONE

VEHICLE IDENTIFICATION NUMBER:

INSURANCE CARRIER   POLICY NUMBER

VEHICLE TYPE | DESCRIBE VEHICLE DAMAGE   SHADE IN DAMAGED AREA
☐ UNK.   ☐ NONE   ☐ MINOR
☐ MOD.   ☐ MAJOR   ☐ ROLL-OVER

DIR OF TRAVEL | ON STREET OR HIGHWAY | SPEED LIMIT

CA _____ DOT _____
CAL-T _____ TCP/PSC _____ MC/MX _____

PARTY 3

DRIVER'S LICENSE NUMBER	STATE	CLASS	AIR BAG	SAFETY EQUIP.	VEH. YEAR	MAKE/MODEL/COLOR	LICENSE NUMBER	STATE

DRIVER ☐ | NAME (FIRST, MIDDLE, LAST)

PEDES-TRIAN ☐ | STREET ADDRESS

OWNER'S NAME ☐ SAME AS DRIVER

PARKED VEHICLE ☐ | CITY/STATE/ZIP

OWNER'S ADDRESS ☐ SAME AS DRIVER

DISPOSITION OF VEHICLE ON ORDERS OF: ☐ OFFICER   ☐ DRIVER   ☐ OTHER

BICY-CLIST ☐ | SEX | HAIR | EYES | HEIGHT | WEIGHT | BIRTHDATE Mo. Day Year | RACE

PRIOR MECHANICAL DEFECTS: ☐ NONE APPARENT   ☐ REFER TO NARRATIVE

OTHER ☐ | HOME PHONE | BUSINESS PHONE

VEHICLE IDENTIFICATION NUMBER:

INSURANCE CARRIER   POLICY NUMBER

VEHICLE TYPE | DESCRIBE VEHICLE DAMAGE   SHADE IN DAMAGED AREA
☐ UNK.   ☐ NONE   ☐ MINOR
☐ MOD.   ☐ MAJOR   ☐ ROLL-OVER

DIR OF TRAVEL | ON STREET OR HIGHWAY | SPEED LIMIT

CA _____ DOT _____
CAL-T _____ TCP/PSC _____ MC/MX _____

PREPARER'S NAME	DISPATCH NOTIFIED ☐ YES ☐ NO ☐ N/A	REVIEWER'S NAME	DATE REVIEWED

Destroy previous editions

c555_b06.frp

185

TRAFFIC COLLISION CODING

Page   of

DATE OF COLLISION (MO. DAY YEAR)	TIME (2400)	NCIC #	OFFICER I.D.	NUMBER

	OWNER'S NAME	OWNER'S ADDRESS	NOTIFIED
PROPERTY DAMAGE			YES
	DESCRIPTION OF DAMAGE		

SEATING POSITION

```
   1 2 3
   4 5 6
   7
```

1 - DRIVER
2 TO 6 - PASSENGERS
7 - STATION WAGON REAR
8 - REAR OCC. TRK. OR VAN
9 - POSITION UNKNOWN
0 - OTHER

OCCUPANTS
A - NONE IN VEHICLE
B - UNKNOWN
C - LAP BELT USED
D - LAP BELT NOT USED
E - SHOULDER HARNESS USED
F - SHOULDER HARNESS NOT USED
G - LAP/SHOULDER HARNESS USED
H - LAP/SHOULDER HARNESS NOT USED
J - PASSIVE RESTRAINT USED
K - PASSIVE RESTRAINT NOT USED

SAFETY EQUIPMENT
L - AIR BAG DEPLOYED
M - AIR BAG NOT DEPLOYED
N - OTHER
P - NOT REQUIRED

CHILD RESTRAINT
Q - IN VEHICLE USED
R - IN VEHICLE NOT USED
S - IN VEHICLE USE UNKNOWN
T - IN VEHICLE IMPROPER USE

M / C BICYCLE- HELMET
DRIVER   PASSENGER
V - NO   X - NO
W - YES   Y - YES

EJECTED FROM VEHICLE
0 - NOT EJECTED
1 - FULLY EJECTED
2 - PARTIALLY EJECTED
3 - UNKNOWN

INATTENTION CODES
A - CELLPHONE HANDHELD
B - CELLPHONE HANDSFREE
C - ELECTRONIC EQUIPMENT
D - RADIO / CD
E - SMOKING
F - EATING
G - CHILDREN
H - ANIMALS
I - PERSONAL HYGIENE
J - READING
K - OTHER

ITEMS MARKED BELOW FOLLOWED BY AN ASTERISK (*) SHOULD BE EXPLAINED IN THE NARRATIVE.

PRIMARY COLLISION FACTOR LIST NUMBER (#) OF PARTY AT FAULT	TRAFFIC CONTROL DEVICES	1	2	3	SPECIAL INFORMATION	1	2	3	MOVEMENT PRECEDING COLLISION
A VC SECTION VIOLATED: CITED YES / NO	A CONTROLS FUNCTIONING				A HAZARDOUS MATERIAL				A STOPPED
	B CONTROLS NOT FUNCTIONING*				B CELL PHONE HANDHELD IN USE				B PROCEEDING STRAIGHT
B OTHER IMPROPER DRIVING*:	C CONTROLS OBSCURED				C CELL PHONE HANDSFREE IN USE				C RAN OFF ROAD
	D NO CONTROLS PRESENT / FACTOR*				D CELL PHONE NOT IN USE				D MAKING RIGHT TURN
C OTHER THAN DRIVER*	TYPE OF COLLISION				E SCHOOL BUS RELATED				E MAKING LEFT TURN
D UNKNOWN*	A HEAD - ON				F 75 FT MOTORTRUCK COMBO				F MAKING U TURN
	B SIDE SWIPE				G 32 FT TRAILER COMBO				G BACKING
	C REAR END				H				H SLOWING / STOPPING
WEATHER (MARK 1 TO 2 ITEMS)	D BROADSIDE				I				I PASSING OTHER VEHICLE
A CLEAR	E HIT OBJECT				J				J CHANGING LANES
B CLOUDY	F OVERTURNED				K				K PARKING MANEUVER
C RAINING	G VEHICLE / PEDESTRIAN				L				L ENTERING TRAFFIC
D SNOWING	H OTHER*:				M				M OTHER UNSAFE TURNING
E FOG / VISIBILITY FT.					N				N XING INTO OPPOSING LANE
F OTHER*:	MOTOR VEHICLE INVOLVED WITH				O				O PARKED
G WIND	A NON - COLLISION								P MERGING
LIGHTING	B PEDESTRIAN								Q TRAVELING WRONG WAY
A DAYLIGHT	C OTHER MOTOR VEHICLE	1	2	3	OTHER ASSOCIATED FACTOR(S) (MARK 1 TO 2 ITEMS)				R OTHER *:
B DUSK - DAWN	D MOTOR VEHICLE ON OTHER ROADWAY								
C DARK - STREET LIGHTS	E PARKED MOTOR VEHICLE				A VC SECTION VIOLATION: CITED YES/NO				
D DARK - NO STREET LIGHTS	F TRAIN				B VC SECTION VIOLATION: CITED YES/NO				
E DARK - STREET LIGHTS NOT FUNCTIONING*	G BICYCLE								SOBRIETY - DRUG PHYSICAL (MARK 1 TO 2 ITEMS)
	H ANIMAL:				C VC SECTION VIOLATION: CITED YES/NO	1	2	3	
ROADWAY SURFACE					D				
A DRY	I FIXED OBJECT:				E VISION OBSCUREMENT:				A HAD NOT BEEN DRINKING
B WET					F INATTENTION*:				B HBD - UNDER INFLUENCE
C SNOWY - ICY	J OTHER OBJECT:				G STOP & GO TRAFFIC				C HBD - NOT UNDER INFLUENCE*
D SLIPPERY (MUDDY, OILY, ETC.)					H ENTERING / LEAVING RAMP				D HBD - IMPAIRMENT UNKNOWN*
ROADWAY CONDITION(S) (MARK 1 TO 2 ITEMS)					I PREVIOUS COLLISION				E UNDER DRUG INFLUENCE*
A HOLES, DEEP RUT*	PEDESTRIAN'S ACTIONS				J UNFAMILIAR WITH ROAD				F IMPAIRMENT - PHYSICAL*
B LOOSE MATERIAL ON ROADWAY*	A NO PEDESTRIANS INVOLVED				K DEFECTIVE VEH. EQUIP.: CITED				G IMPAIRMENT NOT KNOWN
C OBSTRUCTION ON ROADWAY*	B CROSSING IN CROSSWALK - AT INTERSECTION				YES/NO				H NOT APPLICABLE
D CONSTRUCTION - REPAIR ZONE									I SLEEPY / FATIGUED*
E REDUCED ROADWAY WIDTH	C CROSSING IN CROSSWALK - NOT AT INTERSECTION								
F FLOODED*	D CROSSING - NOT IN CROSSWALK				L UNINVOLVED VEHICLE				
G OTHER*:	E IN ROAD - INCLUDES SHOULDER				M OTHER*:				
H NO UNUSUAL CONDITIONS	F NOT IN ROAD				N NONE APPARENT				
	G APPROACHING / LEAVING SCHOOL BUS				O RUNAWAY VEHICLE				

SKETCH

INDICATE NORTH

MISCELLANEOUS

c555_b06.frp

186

POLICE DEPARTMENT

SUPPLEMENTAL REPORT

CRIME TYPE		CASE #	
DATE OCCURRED		PAGE	OF

PERSONS CODE

LIST PERSONS IN FOLLOWING ORDER

VB Victim Business	**V** Victim	**W** Witness	**C** Contacted	**R** Reporting Person	**P** Parent	**M** Mentioned

CODE	#	NAME	LAST, FIRST, MIDDLE	SEX	RACE	AGE	DOB	☐ ☐ ADULT JUV.	INTERPRETER NEEDED! ☐ TYPE—
HOME ADDRESS		NUMBERS, DIR., STREET, CITY, STATE		BUSINESS ADDRESS			NUMBERS, DIR., STREET, CITY, STATE		
HOME PHONE		HOURS	BUSINESS PHONE	HOURS	CDL NUMBER			SS NUMBER	

CODE	#	NAME	LAST, FIRST, MIDDLE	SEX	RACE	AGE	DOB	☐ ☐ ADULT JUV.	INTERPRETER NEEDED! ☐ TYPE—
HOME ADDRESS		NUMBERS, DIR., STREET, CITY, STATE		BUSINESS ADDRESS			NUMBERS, DIR., STREET, CITY, STATE		
HOME PHONE		HOURS	BUSINESS PHONE	HOURS	CDL NUMBER			SS NUMBER	

A Arrestee   **S** Suspect   **JD** Juvenile Detention

CODE	#	NAME	LAST, FIRST, MIDDLE	CHARGE	
RACE	SEX	☐ ADULT ☐ JUV	AGE	DOB	HEIGHT	WEIGHT	HAIR	EYES	BUILD	BOOKING #	BOOKING DATE	BOOKING TIME

HOME ADDRESS	NUMBERS, DIRECTION, STREET, CITY, STATE	HOME PHONE
OCCUPATION & BUSINESS ADDRESS		BUSINESS PHONE
LOCATION ARRESTED	☐ SAME AS LOCATION OF CRIME	DT ARRESTED	TIME ARRESTED
DRIVERS LIC. #/STATE	SOCIAL SECURITY #	CII #	SAPD MUG #	SAPD ID CODE #	☐ UNDOCUMENTED PERSON!
AKA'S	TATTOOS, MARKS, SCARS, ODDITIES & LOCATIONS	CLOTHING AT TIME OF ARREST
BAIL AMOUNT	TIME RELEASED LOCATION HELD	OUTSTANDING WARRANTS/PAROLE OR PROBATION HOLDS

LIST PROPERTY FIRST/EVIDENCE SECOND/SUSPECT INFORMATION THIRD.
LIST SUSPECT SEX, RACE, AGE, HEIGHT, WEIGHT, HAIR, EYES, BUILD, ODDITIES, CLOTHING DESCRIPTION.

INCLUDE WHERE EVIDENCE/PROPERTY BOOKED

ITEM #	QTY.	ARTICLE	BRAND	MODEL #	(COLOR, SIZE, INSCRIPTIONS, CALIBER, MARKS)	SERIAL #	FAIR MARKET $ VALUE

REPORTING OFFICER	ID #	DATE	TIME	AREA	TEAM	WATCH	REPORT REVIEW BY	ID #

DISTRIBUTION   TOTAL COPIES _____   DISTRIBUTION BY/DATE _____

☐ ACCIDENT BOX	☐ COURT LIAISON	☐ ORANGEWOOD	☐ TEAM POLICING	☐ OTHER _____
☐ ANIMAL CONTROL	☐ CRIMES AGAINST PERSON	☐ PROPERTY	☐ TRAFFIC	
☐ AUTO THEFT	☐ CRIME PREVENTION	☐ PROPERTY CRIMES	☐ TRANSPORTATION	☐ OTHER _____
☐ CII	☐ INTELLIGENCE/VICE	☐ SPECIAL/NARCOTICS INV.	☐ OTHER _____	☐ OTHER _____
☐ CALIF. HWY. PATROL	☐ JUVENILE HALL	☐ STATS	☐ OTHER _____	

| | | | NARRATIVE CONTINUATION | | PAGE | OF | | CASE # | |

NARRATIVE CONTINUATION

PAGE ___ OF ___   CASE # ___

LIST PROPERTY FIRST/EVIDENCE SECOND/SUSPECT INFORMATION THIRD.
LIST SUSPECT SEX, RACE, AGE, HEIGHT, WEIGHT, HAIR, EYES, BUILD, ODDITIES, CLOTHING DESCRIPTION.

INCLUDE WHERE EVIDENCE/PROPERTY BOOKED

ITEM #	QTY	ARTICLE	BRAND	MODEL #	(COLOR, SIZE, INSCRIPTIONS, CALIBER, MARKS)	SERIAL #	FAIR MARKET $ VALUE

☐ NARRATIVE CONTINUED

STATEMENT OF PRIVATE PERSON'S (CITIZEN'S) ARREST

Date: _____   Case No: _____

As a **PRIVATE PERSON,** I, _____

               (Surname)   (First)   (Middle)

pursuant to the authority of **Penal Code Sections 834 and 837**, have arrested

_____

       (Surname)   (First)   (Middle)

for _____ ,

       (Indicate Violation)   (Code Section or Ordinance)

a public offense committed in my presence at _____ ,

                                       (Address of Offense)

on _____ at _____

     (Date Offense Committed)   (Time Offense Committed)

I hereby demand that Officer (s) _____ ,

of the   **POLICE DEPARTMENT** receive custody of the above named

arrestee pursuant to Penal Code Sections 847, 849 , and 142.

    I agree to cooperate fully and appear when required at all stages of the proceedings.

    I hereby declare under penalty of perjury that the above information is true and correct to the best of my knowledge and belief. Executed this _____ day of _____ , 20 _____ , at _____ , California.

_____   _____
       (Witness)   (Signature of Person Making Arrest)

_____   _____
       (Witness)   (Address)

                                    _____
                                          (Telephone No.)

NOTICE TO APPEAR

SUPERIOR COURT OF
COUNTY OF   CENTRAL JUSTICE CENTER

☐ MISDEMEANOR

☐ TRAFFIC ☐ NON-TRAFFIC

Date of Violation /	Time	☐ AM ☐ PM	Day of Week	Case #

Name *(First, Middle, Last)*   ☐ Owners Responsibility (Veh. Code § 40001)

Address

City	State	Zip Code

Driver's Lic. #	State	Class	Commercial ☐ Yes ☐ No	Age	Birth Date /

Sex M F	Hair	Eyes	Height	Weight	Other	Description

Veh. Lic. No. or VIN   State

☐ Commercial Vehicle (Veh. Code § 15210b)

Yr. of Veh.	Make	Model	Body Style	Color

☐ Hazardous Material (Veh. Code § 353)

Evidence of financial Responsibility

Registered Owner or Lessee   ☐ Same As Driver

Address   ☐ Same As Driver

City	State	Zip Code

Correctable Violation (Veh. Code § 40610) ☐ Booking Required

Misdemeanor or Infraction (Circle)

Yes	No	Code and Section	Description	
☐	☐			M / I
☐	☐			M / I
☐	☐			M / I
☐	☐			M / I

Speed Approx.	P.F./Max. Spd.	Veh. Lmt.	Safe	Radar	☐ Unit #	☐ Cont. Form Issued

Locations of Violations(s)   City/County of Occurrence

at

☐ ACCIDENT

N
W E
S

TRAFFIC			WEATHER				STREET		LIGHT		
LT.	MED	HVY	CLR	FOG	RAIN	CLDY	DRY	WET	DAY	DSK	DRK

☐ Violations not committed in my presence, declared on information and belief.

I declare under penalty of perjury under the laws of the State of California that the foregoing is true and correct.

		To
/ /	Arresting or Citing Officer	Serial No.	Dates Off
Date	Name of Arresting Officer, if different from Citing Officer	Serial No.	Dates Off

To

WITHOUT ADMITTING GUILT, I PROMISE TO APPEAR AT THE TIME AND PLACE INDICATED BELOW.

X Signature

WHEN: ON THIS DATE: _____ / _____ / _____   TIME 8:00 AM

WHAT TO DO: FOLLOW THE INSTRUCTION ON THE REVERSE.

WHERE:

☐ _____

☐ To be notified ☐ You may arrange with the clerk to appear at a night session of the court.

COURT COPY

DATE		DAY	TIME	TIME MARKED
/ /				

VEH LIC/VIN		STATE	MO/YR

YEAR	MAKE	MODEL	BODY STYLE	COLOR

LOCATION OF VIOLATION   N↑

ON: _____

VIN: _____

IN VIOLATION OF   CODE:

CITY PARKING LOT

☐ 36-131.1 RED ZONE $64	☐ 36-142 TIME LIMIT PKG. HR/2 HRS/GRN ZONE $47	☐ 36-147 PERMIT PKG. $39
☐ 36-131.2 YELLOW ZONE $47	☐ 36-136b PKG. OVER 72 HRS. $63	☐ 36-432.6 OUT OF MARKED STALL $47
☐ 36-131.3 WHITE ZONE	☐ 36-145 OVER 10K G.V.W.R. 2 HR. LIMIT $78	☐ 36-432.11 EXPIRED METER $47
☐ 36-132 NO STOPPING/NO PKG. $68	☐ 36-402.1 EXP. METER $56	NO. _____
☐ 36-145.5 6FT. HIGH VEH. W/IN 100' OF INTER. $69		☐ 41-607e PARK ON LAWN OR LANDSCAPED AREA $69
☐ 36-133 NO PKG. ST. CLEAN. $63	NO. _____ ☐ 36-138a OUT OF MARKED STALL $47	☐ 41-607h COMMERCIAL VEHICLE PROHIBITED IN RES. AREA $69
☐ 36-135a NO PARKING/ALLEY $55	☐ 36-493a PARKING DIST. PERMIT REQUIRED $47	☐ 36-135b STOP, STAND OR PARK VEHICLE W/IN A PARKWAY $55
☐ 36-171 OFF TRUCK ROUTE $92	☐	☐

IN VIOLATION OF   VEHICLE CODE:

☐ 5204 MO. TAB/NO. YR.	☐ 22500f SIDEWALK	☐ 22507.8A DISABLED PKG. $376
☐ 5200 NO LIC. PLATE FRONT/REAR $108	☐ 22500e DRIVEWAY	☐ 22526 INTERSECTION GRIDLOCK $171
☐ 22514 FIRE HYDRANT (WITHIN 15ft) $54	☐ 22500h DBL. PARKING $54	☐ 22500L BLOCKING SIDEWALK WHEELCHAIR ACCESS $258
☐ 22500.1 FIRE LANE $119	☐ 22502a + 18" FROM CURB	☐ 26708.5a TINTED FORWARD WINDOWS $30
	☐ 22500b CROSSWALK	

I CERTIFY UNDER PENALTY OF PERJURY THAT THE FOREGOING IS TRUE AND CORRECT.

OFFICER   BADGE

CS-883   CERTIFICATION OF CORRECTION

Signature	Badge	Agency	Date	Viol

SUSPECTED CHILD ABUSE REPORT

To Be Completed by **Mandated Child Abuse Reporters**
Pursuant to Penal Code Section 11166
PLEASE PRINT OR TYPE

CASE NAME: _____

CASE NUMBER: _____

A. REPORTING PARTY

NAME OF MANDATED REPORTER	TITLE	MANDATED REPORTER CATEGORY
REPORTER'S BUSINESS/AGENCY NAME AND ADDRESS Street City Zip		DID MANDATED REPORTER WITNESS THE INCIDENT? ☐ YES ☐ NO
REPORTER'S TELEPHONE (DAYTIME) ( )	SIGNATURE	TODAY'S DATE

B. REPORT NOTIFICATION

☐ LAW ENFORCEMENT ☐ COUNTY PROBATION ☐ COUNTY WELFARE / CPS (Child Protective Services)	AGENCY	
ADDRESS Street City Zip		DATE/TIME OF PHONE CALL
OFFICIAL CONTACTED - TITLE		TELEPHONE ( )

C. VICTIM
One report per victim

NAME (LAST, FIRST, MIDDLE)	BIRTHDATE OR APPROX. AGE	SEX	ETHNICITY
ADDRESS Street City Zip	TELEPHONE ( )		

PRESENT LOCATION OF VICTIM	SCHOOL	CLASS	GRADE

PHYSICALLY DISABLED? ☐ YES ☐ NO	DEVELOPMENTALLY DISABLED? ☐ YES ☐ NO	OTHER DISABILITY (SPECIFY)	PRIMARY LANGUAGE SPOKEN IN HOME
IN FOSTER CARE? ☐ YES ☐ NO	IF VICTIM WAS IN OUT-OF-HOME CARE AT TIME OF INCIDENT, CHECK TYPE OF CARE: ☐ DAY CARE ☐ CHILD CARE CENTER ☐ FOSTER FAMILY HOME ☐ FAMILY FRIEND ☐ GROUP HOME OR INSTITUTION ☐ RELATIVE'S HOME		TYPE OF ABUSE (CHECK ONE OR MORE) ☐ PHYSICAL ☐ MENTAL ☐ SEXUAL ☐ NEGLECT ☐ OTHER (SPECIFY)
RELATIONSHIP TO SUSPECT		PHOTOS TAKEN? ☐ YES ☐ NO	DID THE INCIDENT RESULT IN THIS VICTIM'S DEATH? ☐ YES ☐ NO ☐ UNK

D. INVOLVED PARTIES

VICTIM'S SIBLINGS

	NAME	BIRTHDATE	SEX	ETHNICITY		NAME	BIRTHDATE	SEX	ETHNICITY
1.					3.				
2.					4.				

VICTIM'S PARENTS/GUARDIANS

NAME (LAST, FIRST, MIDDLE)	BIRTHDATE OR APPROX. AGE	SEX	ETHNICITY
ADDRESS Street City Zip HOME PHONE ( )	BUSINESS PHONE ( )		
NAME (LAST, FIRST, MIDDLE)	BIRTHDATE OR APPROX. AGE	SEX	ETHNICITY
ADDRESS Street City Zip HOME PHONE ( )	BUSINESS PHONE ( )		

SUSPECT

SUSPECT'S NAME (LAST, FIRST, MIDDLE)	BIRTHDATE OR APPROX. AGE	SEX	ETHNICITY
ADDRESS Street City Zip	TELEPHONE ( )		
OTHER RELEVANT INFORMATION			

E. INCIDENT INFORMATION

IF NECESSARY, ATTACH EXTRA SHEET(S) OR OTHER FORM(S) AND CHECK THIS BOX ☐   IF MULTIPLE VICTIMS, INDICATE NUMBER: ____

DATE / TIME OF INCIDENT	PLACE OF INCIDENT

NARRATIVE DESCRIPTION (What victim(s) said/what the mandated reporter observed/what person accompanying the victim(s) said/similar or past incidents involving the victim(s) or suspect)

SS 8572 (Rev. 12/02)   *DEFINITIONS AND INSTRUCTIONS ON REVERSE*

DO NOT submit a copy of this form to the Department of Justice (DOJ). The investigating agency is required under Penal Code Section 11169 to submit to DOJ a Child Abuse Investigation Report Form SS 8583 if (1) an active investigation was conducted and (2) the incident was determined not to be unfounded

WHITE COPY-Police or Sheriff's Department;   BLUE COPY-County Welfare or Probation Department;   GREEN COPY- District Attorney's Office;   YELLOW COPY-Reporting Party

Medical Temp. No:_____

FOR JAIL USE ONLY

PLEASE PRINT OR TYPE

PRE-BOOKING RECORD

BOOKING NUMBER	RECEIVING OFFICER	DATE	SUPPLEMENTAL WARRANTS	HOW MANY
	#			

BKG STATUS

☐ STREET BOOKING	☐ WARRANT	☐ COURT ORDER	☐ OTHER (SPECIFY)
☐ COMMITMENT			

TO BE COMPLETED BY ARRESTING OR TRANSPORTING OFFICER
PLEASE FILL IN ALL OF THE BOXES BELOW THIS LINE PRIOR TO SUBMITTING TO THE RECEIVING GUARD STATION

ARRESTING AGENCY	OCSD AREA OR CONTRACT CITY	AGENCY CASE	DATE & TIME ARRESTED

NAME: LAST	FIRST	MIDDLE

BIRTHDATE	SEX	RACE	HEIGHT	WEIGHT	HAIR	EYES	STATE & COUNTRY OF BIRTH	CITIZENSHIP

AKA	DRIVER'S LICENSE NO. & STATE

JURISDICTION	WARRANT OR CASE NUMBER	BAIL

CHARGE 1	CHARGE 4
CHARGE 2	CHARGE 5
CHARGE 3	CHARGE 6

DNA

☐ DNA COLLECTED BY OFFICER _____	☐ PREVIOUSLY COLLECTED	☐ NOT COLLECTED (EXPLAIN BELOW)

EXPLAIN WHY DNA WAS NOT COLLECTED

OCCUPATION	MARITAL STATUS	SOCIAL SECURITY NUMBER	TELEPHONE NO.

SCARS, MARKS, TATTOOS, AMPS

ADDRESS	CITY	STATE	ZIP

NEXT OF KIN: NAME	RELATIONSHIP	TELEPHONE NO.

ADDRESS	CITY	STATE	ZIP

ARRESTEE EMPLOYER NAME	BUSINESS ADDRESS

OFFICER'S ADDITIONAL INFORMATION—CHECK BOX IF YOU BELIEVE THE ARRESTEE WILL REQUIRE MEDICAL ATTENTION OR SPECIAL MANAGEMENT.
☐ MEDICAL (ILL OR INJURED)　☐ MENTAL　☐ INTOXICATED　☐ PROTECTIVE CUSTODY　☐ HIGH SECURITY

EXPLAIN

ARRESTING OFFICER	MANDATORY FOREIGN CONSULAR NOTIFICATION MADE PER CPC 834c
ID #	☐ YES　☐ NO　☐ N/A

PERMISSION TO USE TELEPHONE AFTER ARREST　(Pursuant to Penal code Section 851.5)
I have been given the opportunity to make three (3) FREE telephone calls within the LOCAL DIALING area, or at MY OWN EXPENSE IF OUTSIDE the Local dialing area.

RECORD OF TELEPHONE CALLS:

Telephone calls DESIRED _____　　Telephone calls COMPLETED _____

Location _____ Date _____ Time _____

Witnessing Officer_____ ID # _____ Agency _____

●❖.F0680-195 (J) (R09/08)　　　　SIGNATURE _____

To be completed upon a physical arrest for any misdemeanor, pursuant to Penal Code Section 853.6.

The person arrested:

1. ☐ was so intoxicated that he could have been a danger to himself or others.

2. ☐ required medical examination or medical care or was otherwise unable to care for his own safety.

3. ☐ was charged with one or more of the offenses listed in section 40302 of the Vehicle Code.
(Note Paragraphs five and eight)

4. ☐ had one or more outstanding arrest warrants issued.

5. ☐ could not provide satisfactory evidence of personal identification.

6. ☐ if released immediately would jeopardize the prosecution of the offense or offenses for which he was arrested or the prosecution of any other offenses.

7. ☐ would be reasonably likely to continue the offense or offenses, or the safety of persons or property would be imminently endangered if immediately released.

8. ☐ demanded to be taken before a magistrate or refused to sign the Notice to Appear.

9. ☐ was not released for one or more of the reasons specified in paragraphs one through eight. Specifically state reason.

_____

_____

SYNOPSIS: (For Officer's Use Only)

_____

_____

_____

_____

_____

_____

_____

_____

_____

_____

_____

_____

_____

_____

Date / Time of Stop: _____	**Driving Under the Influence**	CI # _____
Date / Time of Arrest: _____	**Investigation Report**	Cite# _____
Location of Arrest: _____		Booking#_____

OFFENSE(S) CHARGED

☐ CVC 23152(a)	☐ CVC 23152(b)	☐	☐	☐
☐	☐	☐	☐	☐ Prior DUI Arrest Within 10 years.

COLLISION INFORMATION

Collision Involved: ☐ Yes ☐ No   ☐ Fatal ☐ Injury ☐ Non-injury ☐ Hit-&-Run ☐ Misdemeanor ☐ Felony

ARRESTEE INFORMATION

NAME (last, first, middle)	RACE	SEX	BIRTHDAY	HAIR	EYES	HEIGHT	WEIGHT
RESIDENCE ADDRESS	HOME PHONE			CELL PHONE			
OCCUPATION	EMPLOYER	BUSINESS ADDRESS		WORK PHONE			
DRIVER'S LICENSE NUMBER	STATE	LICENSE STATUS	MISC. #'S (CII#, FBI#, SSN, INS#, ETC.)				

VEHICLE INFORMATION

LICENSE	STATE	MO / YR	VIN#			☐ OPEN CONTAINER
VEH YR	MAKE	MODEL	DOORS	COLOR	VEHICLE DISPOSITION: ☐ IMPOUNDED ☐ STORED ☐ RECOVERED ☐ LEFT @ SCENE	
					☐ RELEASED TO: TOW COMPANY:	

OFFICER / VICTIM / WITNESS / PASSENGER INFORMATION

NAME	☐ OFC. ☐ VIC ☐ WIT ☐ PASS	DOB:	RESIDENCE	RES #
		CDL#		BUS #
NAME	☐ OFC. ☐ VIC ☐ WIT ☐ PASS	DOB:	RESIDENCE	RES #
		CDL#		BUS #
NAME	☐ OFC. ☐ VIC ☐ WIT ☐ PASS	DOB:	RESIDENCE	RES #
		CDL#		BUS #
NAME	☐ OFC. ☐ VIC ☐ WIT ☐ PASS	DOB:	RESIDENCE	RES #
		CDL#		BUS #
NAME	☐ OFC. ☐ VIC ☐ WIT ☐ PASS	DOB:	RESIDENCE	RES #
		CDL#		BUS #
NAME	☐ OFC. ☐ VIC ☐ WIT ☐ PASS	DOB:	RESIDENCE	RES #
		CDL#		BUS #

INTERVIEW QUESTIONS

What have you been drinking?	How much have you been drinking?
What time did you start drinking?	What time did you stop drinking?
Where were you drinking?	With whom have you been drinking?
Where are you now?	☐ Actual location or other:
What time is it now?	☐ Actual time:
Where were you going?	Amount of sleep in the last 24 hours?
How long were you driving this vehicle?	Anything to drink in the last hour?
Where did you start driving from?	When & what have you eaten?
Are you diabetic or epileptic? ☐ Yes ☐ No.	Do you take insulin? ☐ Yes ☐ No. (Pills / injection)
Are you sick or injured? ☐ Yes ☐ No.	Are you under the care of a Doctor or Dentist? ☐ Yes ☐ No.
Did you recently bump your head? ☐ Yes ☐ No.	Recent surgery performed? ☐ Yes ☐ No.
Were you driving this vehicle? ☐ Yes ☐ No. (If no, who was?):	
Do you have any physical impairment? Describe? ☐ Yes ☐ No.	
Have you taken any medicine or drugs recently? ☐ Yes ☐ No.	
Is there anything mechanically wrong with your vehicle? ☐ Yes ☐ No.	
Do you feel the effects of the alcohol? ☐ Yes ☐ No.	

Scale of 1-thru-10, #1 being sober, #10 being intoxicated, how would you rate yourself? (1 2 3 4 5 6 7 8 9 10)

ARRESTING OFFICER (PRINT NAME)	I.D. NUMBER	REVIEWED BY (PRINT NAME)	I.D. NUMBER	DATE

D.U.I. FIELD INTERVIEW

OBJECTIVE SIGNS / APPEARANCE / STANDARDIZED FIELD SOBRIETY TESTS

Breath	Eyes	Speech	Coordination	Appearance	Behavior	Clothing	Following Instructions
☐ Alcohol ☐ Marijuana ☐ Ether/PCP ☐ Strong ☐ Moderate ☐ Weak ☐ None ☐ Other _____ _____ _____	☐ Bloodshot ☐ Red ☐ Watery ☐ Droopy ☐ Dilated ☐ Const. ☐ Clear ☐ Swollen ☐ Glasses ☐ Contacts ☐ Other ____	☐ Slurred ☐ Loud ☐ Soft/Quiet ☐ Mumbled ☐ Spitting ☐ Rapid ☐ Correct ☐ Talkative ☐ Slow ☐ Other	☐ Unsteady Gait ☐ Staggered ☐ Used Support ☐ Fell Down ☐ Fumbled I.D. ☐ Lax Face/Jaw ☐ Dizziness ☐ Drowsiness ☐ Scratching ☐ Tremors ☐ Jerking ☐ Other _____	☐ Unkempt ☐ Vomitus ☐ Hair Mussed ☐ Dry Mouth ☐ Normal ☐ Sweating ☐ Nasal Secretion ☐ Yellow Tongue ☐ Confusion ☐ Injection Wound ☐ Other _____	☐ Anger ☐ Crying ☐ Laughing ☐ Belligerent ☐ Aggressive ☐ Apologetic ☐ Hallucinating ☐ Paranoia ☐ Fluctuating ☐ Violent ☐ Cooperative ☐ Other _____	☐ Disheveled ☐ Stained/Dirty ☐ Wet ☐ Normal ☐ Neat ☐ Unbuttoned ☐ Urinated ☐ Other _____ _____ _____	☐ Good Retention ☐ Fair Retention & Response ☐ Poor Retention & Response ☐ Nuisance ☐ Interrupting ☐ Evasive Answers ☐ Attempts Tests Before / During Instructions ☐ Other _____

Field Sobriety Tests Administered by:
☐ This Officer, or: _____

Test Location: _____
(Surface, Weather, and Lighting)

NYSTAGMUS TEST

<u>HGN Present:</u>   Right Eye - ☐ Yes ☐ No   Left Eye - ☐ Yes ☐ No.   HGN at Maximum Deviation: ☐ Yes ☐ No.

Angle of Onset - ____ ☐ 45° (Degrees).   Vertical Nystagmus: ☐ Yes ☐ No   Lack of Smooth Pursuit ☐ Yes ☐ No.

ONE LEG STAND	WALK AND TURN TEST	(OPTIONAL) Modified Balance	(Optional) Finger to Nose

One Leg Stand:
L R
☐ ☐ Sways while balancing
☐ ☐ Uses arms to balance
☐ ☐ Hopping
☐ ☐ Puts foot down
Type of Footwear

Walk and Turn:
Cannot keep distance _____
Starts too soon _____

	1st Nine	2nd Nine
Stops Walking		
Misses Heel-Toe		
Steps off Line		
Raises Arms		
Actual Steps Taken		

Describe Turn _____   Cannot do Test (explain) _____

INTERNAL CLOCK: Estimated as 30 sec.

Finger to Nose: ○ Right △ Left   Draw lines to spots touched

PRELIMINARY ALCOHOL SCREEN INFORMATION

PAS serial #	Temperature	Results / Test #1	Time	Results / Test #2	Time	Results / Test #3 (If needed)	Time
	☐ °C	0.		0.		0.	

☐ Refer to Santa Ana Police Department PAS Form (attached).

CHEMICAL TEST INFORMATION

☐ Implied Consent Admonishment (23612 (a) (1) (A) VC).

☐ Refused Test(s) 13353(a) VC   (Complete DS 367 Form on Admin "Per Se").

☐ Yes ☐ No   Miranda Advisement given.

☐ Yes ☐ No   Trombetta Advisement given.

Type of Test:	Date & Time:	Location:	Results:	Operator's Name:	Disposition of Sample(s)
☐ Breath					☐ Booked into Evidence Locker #
☐ Blood			Vial #	Collected by:	☐ Retained by Blood Technician

ARRESTING OFFICER (PRINT NAME)	I.D. NUMBER	REVIEWED BY (PRINT NAME)	I.D. NUMBER	DATE

					CASE #

POLICE DEPARTMENT

SHORT FORM
SHOPLIFTING REPORT

PAGE   OF

CRIME SUMMARY

PRIMARY CODE TYPE		SECONDARY CODE TYPE
OTHER CODE TYPE		OTHER CRIME TYPE

A

WHEN OCCURRED	DAY	DATE	TIME	TO	DAY	DATE	TIME	WHEN REPORTED	DAY	DATE	TIME

WHERE OCCURRED NUMBERS, DIRECTION, STREET, APT. #		AREA	TEAM

SUSPECT VEHICLE DESCRIPTION, LIC #, STATE, YR, MK, MODEL, STYLE, COLORS	VICTIM VEHICLE (IF TARGET) LIC #, YR, MAKE, MODEL

PROPERTY	VALUE OF LOSS/RECOVERY	CSI BY	ID #	WERE LATENT PRINTS TAKEN?	Y ☐ N ☐
☐ LOSS ☐ NO LOSS	$ /				

LIST PERSONS IN FOLLOWING ORDER

VB Victim Business   **V** Victim   **W** Witness   **C** Contacted   **R** Reporting Person   **P** Parent   **M** Mentioned

GROUP ALL PERSONS OF THE SAME CODE TOGETHER AND NUMBER EACH PERSON IN THE GROUP.

EXAMPLE: V#1, V#2, V#3, W#1, W#2, P#1, P#2, ETC.

B

CODE	#	NAME	LAST, FIRST, MIDDLE	SEX	RACE	AGE	DOB	☐ ADULT ☐ JUV.	INTERPRETER NEEDED! ☐ TYPE—
HOME ADDRESS				BUSINESS ADDRESS					
HOME PHONE		HOURS	BUSINESS PHONE	HOURS	CDL NUMBER			BOOKING NUMBER	
					SS NUMBER				

CODE	#	NAME	LAST, FIRST, MIDDLE	SEX	RACE	AGE	DOB	☐ ADULT ☐ JUV.	INTERPRETER NEEDED! ☐ TYPE—
HOME ADDRESS				BUSINESS ADDRESS					
HOME PHONE		HOURS	BUSINESS PHONE	HOURS	CDL NUMBER			BOOKING NUMBER	
					SS NUMBER				

CODE	#	NAME	LAST, FIRST, MIDDLE	SEX	RACE	AGE	DOB	☐ ADULT ☐ JUV.	INTERPRETER NEEDED! ☐ TYPE—
HOME ADDRESS				BUSINESS ADDRESS					
HOME PHONE		HOURS	BUSINESS PHONE	HOURS	CDL NUMBER			BOOKING NUMBER	
					SS NUMBER				

C

REPORTING OFFICER	ID#	DATE	TIME	AREA	TEAM	WATCH
REPORT REVIEWED BY	ID#	DATE	TIME			

RECORDS REVIEW _____

DISTRIBUTION   TOTAL COPIES _____   DISTRIBUTION BY/DATE _____

☐ ACCIDENT BOX	☐ COURT LIAISON	☐ ORANGEWOOD	☐ TEAM POLICING	☐ OFCR _____
☐ ANIMAL CONTROL	☐ CRIMES AGAINST PERSON	☐ EVIDENCE	☐ TRAFFIC	☐ OTHER _____
☐ DISTRICT INV.	☐ CRIME PREVENTION	☐ SAPD JAIL	☐ VICE	☐ OTHER _____
☐ CII	☐ INTELLIGENCE	☐ NARCOTICS	☐ ARSON	☐ FAX # _____
☐ JUVENILE HALL	☐ STATS	☐ RAP	☐ SGT. _____	☐ GANGS _____

CONTINUATION	PAGE	OF	CASE #

A Arrestee   S Suspect   JD Juvenile Detention

CODE	#	NAME	LAST, FIRST, MIDDLE		CHARGE

RACE	SEX	☐ ADULT ☐ JUV	AGE	DOB	HEIGHT	WEIGHT	HAIR	EYES	BUILD	BOOKING #	BOOKING DATE	BOOKING TIME

HOME ADDRESS	NUMBERS, DIRECTION, STREET, CITY, STATE	HOME PHONE
OCCUPATION & BUSINESS ADDRESS		BUSINESS PHONE
LOCATION ARRESTED	☐ SAME AS LOCATION OF CRIME	DT ARRESTED / TIME ARRESTED

DRIVERS LIC. # /STATE	SOCIAL SECURITY #	CII #	SAPD MUG #	SAPD ID CODE #	☐ UNDOCUMENTED PERSON!

AKA'S	TATTOOS, MARKS, SCARS, ODDITIES & LOCATIONS	CLOTHING AT TIME OF ARREST
BAIL AMOUNT	TIME RELEASED LOCATION HELD	OUTSTANDING WARRANTS/PAROLE OR PROBATION HOLDS

SUSPECTS ACTIONS:

ENTERED BY:	TOOK PROPERTY FROM:	PROPERTY CONCEALED:	PROPERTY TAKEN BY:
☐ OPEN DOOR	☐ COUNTER/DISPLAY	☐ SALES FLOOR	☐ BOOSTER BAG ☐ PURSE
☐ EMPLOYEE ENT.	☐ CLOTHES RACK	☐ FITTING ROOM	☐ SHOPPING BAG ☐ WEARING
☐ SERVICE ENTRANCE	☐ DRESSING ROOM	☐ BATHROOM	☐ SECRETED ON PERSON
☐ _____	☐ _____	☐ _____	☐ _____

PROPERTY STATUS:	SUSPECT TURNED OVER TO SAPD BY:	RESTITUTION DESIRED BY VICTIM
☐ BOOKED SAPD LOCKER # _____	☐ SECURITY ☐ STORE MANAGER	☐ YES ☐ NO AMOUNT _____
☐ RETAINED BY VICTIM/SECURITY	☐ STORE EMPLOYEE	RESTITUTION MADE BY SUSPECT ☐ YES ☐ NO AMOUNT _____

WITNESS IS: ☐ SECURITY ☐ STORE EMPLOYEE ☐ CITIZEN ☐ OFFICER	VIDEO OF CRIME ☐ YES ☐ NO
AMOUNT OF CURRENCY FOUND ON ARRESTEE	RETAINED BY STORE ☐ YES ☐ NO
CREDIT CARDS FOUND ON ARRESTEE:	

STATEMENTS ATTACHED: ☐ SECURITY ☐ VICTIM ☐ WITNESS ☐ SUSPECT	SIGNED CITIZEN ARREST FORM ☐ YES ☐ NO
SUSPECT ADVISED OF 602 PC ☐ YES ☐ NO BY WHO _____	IN WRITING ☐ YES ☐ NO	STORE 602 ADVISEMENT GIVEN TO SUSPECT ☐ YES ☐ NO

FACTUAL CIRCUMSTANCES – ELEMENTS OF THE OFFENSE:

ADVISED MIRANDA:
☐ YES ☐ NO

ARRESTEE'S STATEMENT: _____

MANDATORY FOR JUVENILES

WAIVED RIGHTS:
☐ YES ☐ NO

DISPOSITION OF ARRESTEE: ☐ WPA # _____	☐ BOOKED AT OCJ ☐ LODGED OCJH ☐ PETITION FILED
☐ RELEASED FOR 849 _____ PC ☐ RELEASED TO PARENTS – NO FURTHER POLICE ACTION	☐ RELEASED PENDING FILING BY D.A.
	☐ NARRATIVE CONTINUED

IDENTITY THEFT REPORT

CASE NUMBER		

DISTRICT	GRID	PAGE	OF

OFFENSE	DESCRIPTION
CPC 530.5 ☐	ID THEFT ONLY – Victim resides in _____ , but all fraud activity is occurring in other jurisdictions. (USE VICTIM'S HOME ADDRESS IN "REPORTING ADDRESS" BOX)
CPC 530.5 ☐	ID THEFT & FRAUDULENT ACTIVITY – Victim resides in _____ & all/some fraud activity occurring in _____ (USE _____ ADDRESS WHERE FRAUDULENT ACTIVITY OCCURRED IN "REPORTING ADDRESS" BOX)
REPORTING ADDRESS (SEE ABOVE)	BUSINESS NAME (IF ANY) _____ REPORTING ADDRESS (INCLUDE ZIP CODE)

DATE FRAUD BEGAN	DAY	DATE	TIME	DATE OF LAST FRAUD ACTIVITY	DAY	DATE	TIME
DATE DISCOVERED	DAY	DATE	TIME	WHEN REPORTED	DAY	DATE	TIME

NOTE: VICTIM IS PERSON WHOSE IDENTITY WAS USED

CODE	#	VICTIM NAME LAST, FIRST, MIDDLE (OR BUSINESS NAME)	SEX	RACE	AGE	DATE OF BIRTH	INTERPRETER NEEDED ☐ TYPE -
V	1						

HOME ADDRESS NUMBERS, DIR., STREET, CITY, STATE, ZIP	BUSINESS ADDRESS NUMBERS, DIR., STREET, CITY, STATE, ZIP	CAN ID SUSPECT? YES ☐ NO ☐

BUSINESS PHONE	HOME PHONE	SOCIAL SECURITY NUMBER	CDL NUMBER

ID VERIFIED BY OFFICER? Y ☐ N ☐   VICTIM WILLING TO PROSECUTE? Y ☐ N ☐   VICTIM WILL TESTIFY Y ☐ N ☐

OTHER POLICE REPORTS FILED? Y ☐ N ☐ AGENCY/CASE #:

CREDIT BUREAUS NOTIFIED? Y ☐ N ☐   LIST:

FRAUDULENT ACCOUNTS

	COMPANY NAME / ADDRESS	ACCOUNT NUMBER / AMOUNT OF CHARGES	DATE OPEN / DATE CLOSED	PHONE NUMBER / FAX NUMBER	AFFIDAVIT FILED?
1					Y ☐ N ☐
2					Y ☐ N ☐
3					Y ☐ N ☐
4					Y ☐ N ☐
5					Y ☐ N ☐

Suspect Photograph Available?   YES ☐ NO ☐ UNK ☐   Video Available? YES ☐ NO ☐ UNK ☐ (DETAIL IN NARRATIVE)
Is Suspect Known to Victim?   YES ☐ NO ☐ UNK ☐   Relationship:

BRIEFLY DESCRIBE MERCHANDISE, SERVICES, CASH or OTHER BENEFIT RECEIVED BY SUSPECT.	DOLLAR VALUE OF ACTUAL LOSS (IF ANY)

REPORTING OFFICER	ID #	DATE	TIME	DISTRICT	WATCH	REPORT REVIEW BY	ID #

RECORDS REVIEW _____   TOTAL COPIES _____   DISTRIBUTION BY/DATE: _____

DISTRIBUTION: ☐ COURT LIAISON ☐ DISTRICT INV ☐ OTHER _____

IDENTITY THEFT REPORT – CONTINUATION PAGE

CI #:

PAGE ____ OF ____

S – SUSPECT A – ARRESTEE JD—JUVENILE DETENTION (List additional persons on Name Continuation forms.)

CODE	#	LAST, FIRST, MIDDLE		SEX	RACE	AGE	DATE OF BIRTH	CHARGES

HAIR	EYES	HEIGHT	WEIGHT	CDL/ID NUMBER	SOCIAL SECURITY #	CII NUMBER	FBI NUMBER

HOME ADDRESS	NUMBERS, DIR., STREET, CITY, STATE, ZIP	BUSINESS ADDRESS	NUMBERS, DIR., STREET, CITY, STATE, ZIP

HOME PHONE	BUSINESS PHONE	BOOKING/CITE NUMBER	LOCATION BOOKED/CITED

AKA'S	TATTOOS, MARKS, SCARS, ODDITIES	CLOTHING AT TIME OF ARREST

Miranda Advised? YES ☐ NO ☐   Waived YES ☐ NO ☐ Attorney Requested YES ☐ NO ☐

VEHICLE DESCRIPTION	LICENSE NUMBER	STATE	YEAR	MAKE	MODEL	TYPE	COLOR	DISTINGUISHING DETAILS

REMEMBER:
- Provide victim with Identity Theft Pamphlet and phone number for ID Theft Registry (888-880-0240)
- Advise victim additional information will be mailed to their listed address
- If possible, attach photocopy of victim's drivers' license or other valid photo ID

EVIDENCE (Attach photocopies of ANY documents to this report):

1
2
3

Location booked: ADDITIONAL EVIDENCE ☐

NARRATIVE:

NARRATIVE CONTINUED ☐

REPORTING OFFICER	ID #	DATE	TIME	DISTRICT	WATCH	REPORT REVIEW BY	ID #

Spelling Words

With the advent of text messaging, email, and spell check the ability of young Americans to spell correctly has eroded rapidly. Spelling can enhance or detract from the credibility of a police report. District attorneys, defense attorneys, judges and even juries will make assumptions about your competency by simply reading your police report. It is a good practice when texting to write the entire message and look up words in a dictionary when necessary; *never* guess how to spell a word. If any word gives you particular trouble, write it down a few dozen times and you will never forget it!

Law enforcement uses the same terminology over and over again. Keep a list of difficult words for quick reference while writing your report. Eventually, you will memorize all of these words and no longer need the reference list.

The following pages contain words commonly utilized in law enforcement:

List # 1

ABANDONED	ANTAGONIZE	AUTOMATIC
ADDICTED	APOLOGIZE	AVENUE
ADJUSTABLE	APPEARANCE	BATON
ADEQUATE	APPROXIMATELY	BARBITURATE
ADJACENT	ARGUMENT	BEHAVIOR
ADMINISTRATIVE	ARRESTED	BENEFICIAL
ADMISSIBLE	ARRIVAL	BELLIGERENT
ADMONISH	ARSENAL	BECAUSE
AFFIDAVIT	ARSENIC	BARREL
AFRAID	ARTIFICIAL	BARRICADE
AGENCY	ASPIRIN	BEVERAGE
AGGRESSOR	ATTACK	BICYCLE
ALCOHOL	AUTHORIZE	BINOCULARS
ALIAS	ABSOLUTE	BOISTEROUS
ALIBI ALLEY	ACCELERATE	BOULEVARD
AMATEUR	ASSAULT	BRUISE
AMBULANCE	ASSISTANCE	BUREAU
AMMUNITION	ACCESSORY	BURGLARY
AMNESIA	ACETYLENE	CONFESSION
AMPHETAMINE	ACHIEVEMENT	CONSPIRACY
AMUSEMENT	ACQUAINTANCE	CONDITION
ANALYSIS	ACCIDENTAL	COMPLETED
	ATTEMPT	CONVULSION

List # 2

COMPLAINT	COLLIDE	DEXEDRINE
COUNTERFEIT	COLLISION	DIAGRAM
CALENDAR	CORONER	DIAMOND
CALIBER	COMMAND	DILATED
CAPTURE	COMMUNICATE	DIMENSION
CARBURETOR	COMPETENT	DISARRANGED
CASHIER	COMMERCIAL	DISCREPANCY
CASUALTY	CRUELTY	DISEASE
CEMETERY	CRUISING	DISPATCHED
CERTIFICATE	CYLINDER	DISPERSE
CONDEMN	DANGEROUS	DISTRICT
CORROBORATE	DAUGHTER	DOUBTFUL
CONCENTRATION	DEADLY	DUPLICATE
CONSTITUTION	DECEASED	EMBEZZLEMENT
CHAUFFEUR	DEFECATE	EMERGENCY
CHEVROLET	DEFENSE	ENFORCEMENT
CHILDREN	DELIBERATE	ENVIRONMENT
CHRYSLER	DEMONSTRATION	EQUIPMENT
CITIZEN CIVIL	DEPARTMENTAL	ESTABLISH
CLIENTELE	DESCEND	EVIDENCE
COERCION	DESCRIPTION	EXAGGERATE
COINCIDENCE	DETAILS	EXCEPTION
COLLABORATE	DETAINED	EXHAUSTED
	DETRIMENTAL	ELIGIBLE

List # 3

EMBARRASS	IMMEDIATELY	LEISURE LICENSE
EXHIBITION	IMPORTANT	LIEUTENANT
EXTORTION	INCOHERENT	LIFEGUARD
FAMILIAR	INCONSISTENT	LIQUOR
FICTITIOUS	INCORRIGIBLE	MACHETE
FINGERPRINT	INDECENT	MAINTAIN
FORCIBLE	INFORMANT	MAINTENANCE
FOREIGN	INFORMATION	MALICIOUS
FORGERY	INNOCENT	MANEUVER
FOUND	INTELLIGENCE	MANNEQUIN
FRACTURE	INTERROGATE	MANSLAUGHTER
FRAUDULENT	INTERSECTION	MARTIAL
GAUGE	INTERVIEW	MATERIAL
GENERATOR	INTOXICATION	MEASUREMENT
GOVERNMENT	INVESTIGATE	MILLIMETER
GUARDIAN	IRRELEVANT	MISCHIEF
HEIGHT	JEOPARDY	MISDEMEANOR
HEROIN	JEWELRY	MODEL
HYDRAULIC	KNIFE	MUSTACHE
HABITS	KNUCKLES	MUTUAL
HALLUCINATION	LABORATORY	NECESSITY
HANDKERCHIEF	LACERATION	NEGLIGENCE
IDENTIFICATION	LANGUAGE	NEITHER
ILLEGITIMATE	LEGITIMATE	

List # 4

NOTICEABLE	PARAPHERNALIA	REFERRED
OBNOXIOUS	PARTIALLY	RELEASE
OBSCURE	PARTICIPATE	RESISTANCE
OBSTACLE	PEDESTRIAN	RESTAURANT
OCCASION	PENITENTIARY	REVOKED
OCCURRENCE	PERIMETER	RECOMMEND
OFFENSE	PERMANENT	REVOLVER
OFFENSIVE	PRIVATE	SCENE
OFFICER	PROCESS	SCISSORS
OFFICIAL	PROFESSIONAL	SEARCH
OPERATION	PROHIBITED	SEIZE
OPERATOR	PROPERTY	SELECTIVE
OPPORTUNITY	PROSECUTION	SEPARATED
PERSONNEL	PROSTITUTION	SERGEANT
PERSPIRATION	PUNITIVE	SILHOUETTE
PERVERSION	PURSUIT	SIMILAR
PHYSICAL	QUARANTINE	SITUATION
PISTOL	QUARREL	SOLICITOR
PORNOGRAPHIC	QUESTION	SPANISH
POSSESSION	QUESTIONING	SPECIMEN
POSSIBLE	QUIET	SUSPICIOUS
PRESENCE	RACIAL	STANDARD
PRISONER	RECKLESS	SUBTLE
PARALLELED	RECOGNIZE	SUICIDE

205

List # 5

SURRENDER	TRANSMIT	VIAL
TATTOO	TRANSPORT	VICIOUS
TECHNIQUE	TRESPASSING	VIETNAMESE
TELEVISION	TROUBLE	VIOLATION
TOBACCO	UNCONSCIOUS	VISIBLE
TOURNIQUET	UNDERSTAND	WAIVER
TRAFFIC	UNIFORM	WATCHED
TRANSACTION	UNIQUE	WEIGHT
TRANSLATOR	URINATE	

Conclusion

Never stop learning! Read and study every book in the Police and Fire Publishing series and you will be exponentially more prepared than you would be with any other method.

WWW.POLICEANDFIREPUBLISHING.COM